Pagan Portals

The Muses

Calling to Creativity & Inspiration

What People Are Saying About

The Muses: Calling to Creativity & Inspiration

This book has something for anyone who feels the need for creative inspiration. The Muses are the Ancient Greek goddesses of poetry, song, music, and dance, and have long been called upon by writers, musicians and anyone engaged in the arts. In *Pagan Portals – The Muses*, Irisanya Moon offers a well-researched look at their history and mythology, and offers practical ways to honour them and ask for their aid. You can meet them via trance and meditation; work with them via writing, painting, or music; perform a ritual in their honour; or simply get to know them better and learn the stories told about them. Irisanya Moon also looks at the role of the Muses in our contemporary world and ways we can find inspiration in everyday life.
Lucya Starza, author of the Pagan Portals books *Candle Magic, Poppets and Magical Dolls, Scrying,* and *Rounding the Wheel of the Year*, as well as the novel *Erosion*

Known to inspire people in the arts and sciences, the Muses also are said to inspire us in order to create, to dream new beginnings, and to bring more joy and happiness into our lives. In *Pagan Portals – The Muses: Calling to Creativity & Inspiration*, Irisanya Moon shares with the reader ways of connecting to these nine Greek Goddesses who can inspire and guide us in becoming more proactive in creating a world that we desire.
Frances Billinghurst, author of *Encountering the Dark Goddess: A Journey into the Shadow Realms, Contemporary Witchcraft: Foundational Practices for a Magical Life* and *On Her Silver Rays: A Guide to the Moon, Myth and Magic*

Beings of myth and adventure, the Muses are often overlooked by modern writers and magic workers. No longer, as Irisanya Moon offers us a glorious paean to these inspiring, wise, and creative Beings. Muses is a rich resource reminding us that creativity is an energetic state powered by curiosity that manifests within seemingly mundane actions, every click of a button, or stroke of a brush.
Lisa McSherry, author of *A Traveler's Guide to Making Magic*

Pagan Portals

The Muses

Calling to Creativity & Inspiration

Irisanya Moon

London, UK
Washington, DC, USA

First published by Moon Books, 2026
Moon Books is an imprint of Collective Ink Ltd.,
Unit 11, Shepperton House, 89 Shepperton Road, London, N1 3DF
office@collectiveinkbooks.com
www.collectiveinkbooks.com
www.moon-books.net

For distributor details and how to order please visit the 'Ordering' section on our website.

ISBN: 978 1 80341 746 2
978 1 80341 974 9 (ebook)
Library of Congress Control Number: 2024948557

A CIP catalogue record for this book is available from the British Library.

Design: Lapiz Digital Services

UK: Printed and bound by CPI Group (UK) Ltd, Croydon, CR0 4YY
US: Printed and bound by Thomson-Shore, 7300 West Joy Road, Dexter, MI 48130

Contents

If we want to dream of a new world, we need all the help we can get. We need divine support to see beyond what we know and what we think is possible. The Muses can offer us inspiration through poetry, history, astronomy, comedy, dance, and music. With their relentless creativity, the Muses not only inspire artists, but also those who want to create new structures and new visions of sustainable, supportive communities. With their guidance, we can widen our thinking and conceive of solutions to serve the emerging needs of the world. Connecting and reconnecting to inspiration fosters hope and courage, and the Muses are ready to pass on their knowledge, a knowing that only comes from having seen all that has ever happened.

Invocation to the Muses[1]

Daughters of Mnemosyne,
daughters of thundering Zeus,
Pierian Muses,
renowned and illustrious,
many-shaped and beloved
of the mortals you visit,
you give birth to unblemished virtue
in every discipline,
you nourish the soul,
you set thought aright
as you become leaders,
as you become mistresses of the mind's power.
Sacred and mystic rites
you taught to mortals,
Kleio, Euterpe,
Thaleia, Melpomene,
Terpsichore, Erato,
Polymnia, Ourania,
mother Kalliope,
mighty goddess Hagne.
Do come to the initiates, O goddesses,
in your manifold holiness,
do bring glory and emulation
that is lovely and sung by many.

Orphic Hymn LXXVI: To the Muses, The Orphic Hymns, translated by Apostolos N. Athanassakis and Benjamin M. Wolkow

Acknowledgments

Thank you to Trevor Greenfield for your support and encouragement. I've been writing with Moon Books since 2013, and it's been a journey of growth, challenge, and magick. Thanks is not enough.

Because I haven't done this in a book yet, I want to take this moment to thank my friend, Jarrah. Many ideas have been borne out of conversations with him, including my prior book on Hestia and this one. And others to come. You're a Muse too, my friend, a beloved of another hemisphere and a wild heart of truth-telling. Thank you for the love spell you are.

The Muses have been in my life since my first breath. Nameless until recently, but a constant figure in sleepless nights and early mornings. You have filled notebooks and digital files with your inspirations. And I follow your gentle nudges, the feelings I recognize as your presence. The one that sits close to melancholy but is the sensation of creativity curling around my body, asking me to stay with it a little longer.

I will listen, create, and return to you for all my days.

Author's Notes

[T]here are singers and harpers upon the earth; but princes are of Zeus, and happy is he whom the Muses love: sweet flows speech from his mouth. For although a man has sorrow and grief in his newly-troubled soul and lives in dread because his heart is distressed, yet, when a singer, the servant of the Muses, chants the glorious deeds of men of old and the blessed gods who inhabit Olympus, at once he forgets his heaviness and remembers not his sorrows at all; but the gifts of the goddesses soon turn him away from these.

Theogony, Hesiod, Pg 95, translated by
Hugh G. Evelyn-White

Before you begin reading about the Muses, I want to locate you in the way I approach these books about deities and essential figures in Greek mythology. This will help you better understand my perspective and how it informs the following text.

If you've read other books by me, you will notice I use 'godds' instead of 'gods' when discussing deities. My friend, Urania, uses this word, and I adopted it. I use it to move away from a binary gendered experience of deities. And while I will still use pronouns to refer to godds, you might notice that I may not do this with the Muses. After all, why would inspiration be limited to one gender?

Additionally, you will notice many spellings for the names of the Muses. I have tried to be consistent in the areas of my writing but have left the different spellings as found in source texts, stories, and other materials. I believe they are similar enough to identify the particular Muse, focusing on the Olympian Muses.

Finally, I also want to state that my perspective of the godds is informed by my life experience, access to resources, and interpretation of the writings. My goal in every book is to open to curiosity and to offer multiple perspectives and exercises to build relationships with deities and energies. Building relationships with godds requires a commitment to staying open to other perspectives, which can shift and change just as we move and change in our life experiences.

Better said, my thoughts are not meant to be a final answer to the Muses or any godd. But one way in which I hope to be helpful and supportive in your journey. Let inspiration come to you as it does.

Introduction

Thus thereafter the whole day long until the sun went under
they [the godds on Olympus] feasted, nor was anyone's hunger denied a fair portion,
nor denied the beautifully wrought lyre in the hands of Apollo
nor the anitiphonal sweet sound of the Muses singing.

The Iliad, Homer, Book One, lines 60-604,
translated by Richmond Lattimore

At the start of many stories of the Greek godds is a reference to the Muses. The narrator asks the Muses to tell the stories of the godds, to regale the audience with the details of love and adventure. These beings are celebrated for their wisdom and their memories of what happened. I appreciate the idea of calling to inspiration itself to tell the stories, as they are likely more reliable narrators, more so than the participants and the inconsistent humans or deities.

In a world where creativity is celebrated and consumed, the Muses show their faces to us daily. And with every click of a button and every note in an app, we bring forth what the Muses might have to tell and show us. While the Muses may not be introducing all we see in our lives, their influence is difficult to ignore.

While you may not consider yourself to be an artistic being or someone who can draw or sculpt or write, you are inspired to bring forth something into this world. And I believe this inspiration fosters hope in the most challenging times. When I can see the world as a place filled with inspiration, I can also believe in the possibility that moments of frustration and confusion are contractions of creation.

Every day, we create something new. It might not be a blockbuster or measurable by capitalism, but something new arrives each day, whether it is how you see a person or a problem, or both. Maybe it is in how you look at your partner differently or take a breath before responding to a bot online. Each day offers the possibility of showing up for what the Muses desperately want us to hear and know.

> *Show up, show up, show up, and after a while the muse shows up, too.*
>
> Isabel Allende

I can't remember how I began to understand the Muses, as it seems to be two memories competing in my mind. One memory is of sitting in a conference hall, listening to Thomas Moore speak about embracing your daimon, an energy that was waiting for you to hear so it could tell you what you were on this earth to do. Another memory is of a TED talk by Elizabeth Gilbert about how creativity is something that shows up for you when you show up for it. (Or maybe the Muses had sent me many messages, and it took a few for me to listen.)

What's also true is that I met the Muses in the most profound depression of my life. I met them when I was miserable, and all I could do to keep myself on the planet was write. I wrote in a notebook in my car before and after work, trying to talk myself into making it through one more day. I wrote notes about how I deserved better in my life and how angry I was at the circumstances I found myself in.

I was in jobs I didn't like, not making enough money, not feeling settled or seen, and I was afraid my life would always be that way. I cried myself to sleep and awake. I was in my mid-twenties, newly married, and life was much harder than I thought it should be. I got a well-paid job at one point, and I thought that was the ticket to happiness. After all, I had everything and wore a suit every day. I mattered. But my boss was a misogynist and a jerk. He scolded me, tore away my boundaries, and I became a well-paid, depressed person.

After weeks of writing out my rage on page after page of a small pink notebook, I decided I needed to leave. I needed to leave the 'normal' working world behind and write. That was what I was supposed to do. For the years I devoted myself to writing, I was myself, embodied, and alive. I wanted that. I needed that.

Emboldened by a weekend of psychedelics, I went to work on a Monday, completed the payroll, and dropped it off at HR with my resignation letter. I had written the letter weeks before, but this was the day I turned it in with my keys and never looked back. I let my husband know I had quit on the way home. And I didn't know how to 'be a writer,' but I would figure it out.

And I did. I've been a professional writer across genres since 2005.

I could say the Muses made me do it. I could say all roads were always leading me to follow inspiration, but the real story is that I trusted inspiration and acted on it. It was not easy. It is still not easy. But it is worth it.

Who I Wrote This Book For

Each book I have written up to this point has included a central theme or message. And a book on the Muses might seem straightforward and about creativity. While this is a large part of this book, I also want to make sure you know this:

Creativity is an energy more than an end product

While the Muses might have certain 'kinds' of creativity associated with them, remember it's not necessarily about doing as they do. It's more about being inspired by their gifts to unfold your unique kind of creativity. (To reassure you further, I will not pick up a lyre any time soon.)

Everyone has inherent creativity

I believe we all have something unique to offer to the world, even if our backgrounds are similar or someone else has done what we can do. Our unique stories offer perspectives only we can have and share from our hearts.

Creativity arrives alongside curiosity

At the time of writing the first draft of this book, President Joe Biden had stepped down from running for the US presidency, endorsing Vice President Kamala Harris to run on the Democratic ticket. Many people in the US, where I presently live, are inspired by this change, while others are not. I'm not going to get into the politics of this moment (as it will be much different by the time this book comes into the world), but what does seem to be true right now is that curiosity about what might happen next is fueling creativity in online conversations, social media posts, and, yes, memes.

Open to inspiration, and you open doors

I don't necessarily want my story to inspire you to quit your job. But I will say that my life has taught me that the more I open to inspiration and the magick of inspiration, the more I have been able to step into a life that feels like the right fit for me. And suppose a lot of people were to step into that feeling too. In that case, I imagine a world that can dismantle systems of oppression, find and implement solutions to climate change, become better humans to each other, and radically remember the power of collective inspiration.

Before introducing you to the Muses, I want you to remember this. Much like fate, the Muses are everywhere, and while you might not get a direct message from their mouths or instruments, you are led by inspiration at every moment. You don't need a bright light or a dramatic life situation to know the presence of Muses; you have met inspiration by picking up this book.

That's the Muses. When you arrive, bags fully packed, for a trip into what comes next, a shift into a new path you did not dream of before.

Chapter 1
Encountering the Muses

> *Come now, from the Muses let us begin, who with their singing delight the great mind of Zeus the father in Olympus, as they tell of what is and what shall be and what was aforetime, voices in unison. The words flow untiring from their mouths, and sweet, and the halls of their father, loud-thundering Zeus, rejoice at the goddesses' clear voice spread abroad, and the peak of snowy Olympus rings, and the mansions of the gods. Making divine utterance, they celebrate first in their song the august family of gods, from the beginning, those whom Earth and broad Heaven begot, and the gods that were born from them, givers of blessings. Second they sing of Zeus, father of gods and men, how far the highest of the gods he is, and the greatest in power. And again they sing of the family of men and of powerful Giants to delight the mind of Zeus in Olympus, those Olympian Muses, daughters of Zeus the aegis-bearer.*
>
> Theogony, Hesiod, Pg 4, translated by M.L. West

The Muses celebrate the godds of Olympus, which makes sense in Greek magick and mythology. These goddesses with clear voices sing praises of the godds across the lands. They are trusted to make music and delight the king of the godds, Zeus.

To encounter the Muses can be hearing their songs on the wind. Or they might arrive as a hunch or an idea. They might travel to the space of your frustration and bring you a new perspective that shifts your emotions and responses. While they are often portrayed as traditional Greek goddesses in white and carrying symbols of their gifts, they are also the movement of thought and a whisper of a song you can't stop singing.

Encountering these beings can seem less challenging than other deities, as they seem part of the cultural narrative across groups and times. In my experience, the Muses are often just 'the muse,' living collectively as one being informed by all the qualities of the nine most often found in art and text.

And you have likely encountered them, even without a name or proper introduction. But as they are beings who have introduced the godds, meeting them and introducing ourselves seems polite and kind.

Calling versus Being Called

One of the most common questions I see in working with deities or any energies is whether you need to wait to be called or you can call on a deity. I'm not in charge of the proper procedures, and I think everyone is different in how they begin, create, and maintain relationships with godds.

To me, something about the Muses can feel like water, which is hard to hold or name as a form. While there are images of the Muses, they exist more as an experience, sometimes more as a memory than as an interaction. But maybe that's just me.

In my study of the Greek godds, calling to the Muses was/is commonplace. They are used to being named in rituals and stories. You might decide that the work of this book right now is for you to call out to those Muses or just one Muse that seems to be the best fit for your life and needs.

At the same time, there might be a Muse or multiple Muses who seem to be showing up in your life now or have already shown up in the past. With this experience, answering that call with more dedicated practice and devotional work might feel right. When honoring and committing to inspiration, trust what feels right.

How to Use This Book

I hesitate to tell anyone how to do anything, as what you do with the godds is your business. And I know starting a relationship with a deity, let alone a group of them, can be intimidating at first. What I find most helpful is to read a book and see what arrives for me during that time – both in the reading and when I'm not reading. How do I feel? What am I motivated to do? What shifts? What am I inspired to shift?

I include some exercises in this book to help you connect with the Muses, so you can do those as they are listed or choose ones that seem more helpful to your current state of mind. The last chapter is about building a relationship with the Muses, which you will already be doing just by spending time with them in the prior chapters. But that chapter will outline basic steps for solid relationship-building, including how to navigate confusion and unclear messages.

Most people will read from start to finish, and the book is set up for that. And if you want to skip right to the end, you can. Reading about the Muses' history and the 'facts' is a great way to have a solid foundation before doing exercises, but if you're inspired to follow another order, do that!

No matter what you do, it can help to journal about what you experience, what happens in your life, and how you feel. I find journaling to be a great reference when I'm further along, as it shows me just how far I have come, and sometimes my older ideas are the missing pieces I need for a present-day question.

And if you're not into writing things down, you can also create art or dance or sing or close your eyes and settle into a land where the Muses stand up and sing your story to the godds again and again.

Trance Work: Meeting the Muses

One of the ways I reach out to a godd is through trance. This is a great way to meet and offers a tool to interact with a godd throughout our relationship. My training in Reclaiming Witchcraft informs my trance style, so it is different from meditation, journeying, or path-working, from my understanding.

When I lead a trance, I begin with an induction that helps to bring the trance traveler into their body and into a safe state of being. This can be a guided relaxation, a description of a staircase, or other imagery that helps bring someone into a place ready to open to another state of consciousness.

From there, I will describe a journey to the Muses without telling you exactly what you will experience. My trance style is to keep it open-ended so anyone can have the experience they need, versus being prescriptive. That said, not all trances will be life-changing, soul-rocking experiences. Sometimes, you might not know what you experienced or be confused. Other times, you might not feel you had any experience but notice something pop up in a dream later.

Any experience you have is legitimate and perfect for you. You don't need to see bright colors or dramatic scenes (I never do). You don't need to come back with all the answers. There is no 'right' way to do this; there is only your way.

You can choose to record this trance ahead of time, or you can read it a few times and lead yourself. You might share this with a friend or partner who might read the words to you.

I try to keep the language open-ended and trauma-informed. You don't have to finish a trance if it doesn't feel right for you. And know that you can change my words if you think there is something that might serve you better.

Ready?

Find a comfortable position in a room where you will not be interrupted. You can lie down, sit, or walk if that feels supportive. And you can change your mind during the trance. The idea is to help your body feel comfortable and present without falling asleep. But if you fall asleep, this is fine. The trances where I have fallen asleep, sometimes, are more potent.

Once you are in a comfortable position, close your eyes or have your eyes half-closed. You can have your eyes open and focus on a soothing item in your space, if that helps you, e.g., a candle flame, a water fountain, etc.

You might notice your breath, how it moves your chest or stomach up and down. You don't need to change it into something else. Notice what it feels like and what it does as you pay attention to air moving in and out of your lungs, nose, and mouth.

Notice how your body easily settles. And if you're not feeling settled, maybe take your mind back to a time when you felt completely, utterly safe and grounded. With that memory, you can remind yourself that you are able to settle and ground, and you will do that when you are ready.

Allow your awareness to settle by your feet and ankles. What do you notice? There is no need to change or fix anything. Notice what lives in those spaces right now. If there is anything that doesn't need to be present, allow it to sink, drop, and fall away.

(Pause for 10 seconds.)

Notice your awareness rise to your calves, knees, and thighs. What do you notice? Again, there is no need to change or fix; just notice what lives here right now. And if there is anything that doesn't need to be present, allow it to sink, drop, and fall away.

(Pause for 10 seconds.)

Let awareness travel to the space between your hips, maybe it feels good to have your awareness swirl around in this space. What do you notice? There is no need to change or fix anything; notice what lives here right now. And if there is anything that doesn't need to be here, allow it to sink, drop, and fall away.

(Pause for 10 seconds.)

Easily, so easily, your awareness can travel to your solar plexus and the place of digestion. What do you notice? As always, there is no need to change or fix; just notice what lives here. And if there is anything that doesn't need to be here, allow it to sink, drop, and fall away.

(Pause for 10 seconds.)

Again, your awareness travels to your ribs, lungs, and creative heart. What do you notice? There is no need to change or fix anything; just notice what lives here right now. And if there is anything that doesn't need to be here right now, allow it to sink, drop, and fall away.

(Pause for 10 seconds.)

So easily, your awareness can travel to your shoulders and along each arm – from shoulder to elbow to wrist, fingers and thumbs. What do you notice? There is no need to change or fix anything; just notice what lives here. And if there is anything that doesn't need to be here right now, allow it to sink, drop, and fall away.

(Pause for 10 seconds.)

Calmly and easily, your awareness can travel to your neck and jaw, and then to the space of your eyes, mouth, and forehead, all the way to the top of your head and the space that was soft when you were born. What do you notice? There is no need to change or fix; notice what lives here. And if there is anything that doesn't need to be here right now, allow it to sink, drop, and fall away.

(Pause for 10 seconds.)

Just to be sure, I invite you to scan your body to see if anything else needs to drop, sink, and fall away. It can do this so easily.

(Pause for 10 seconds.)

As you feel present and grounded and safe and calm, I invite you to expand your awareness from the crown of your head. Maybe you open your magickal eye here, or you roll out your awareness like a blanket to the edges of the horizon. You can choose what makes sense to expand your knowing and drop into wisdom.

In this space, you might notice a path. What does the path look like? What does it feel like? Where is it located? What is its direction? How does it curve? How do you travel on it? Do you float above? Follow this path that calls to you and wants you to take a journey to the Muses.

You can take time here to travel, as you like. Perhaps you want to explore nature or the waters or the structures or the crystals. This is the path that's laid out for you, and you get to decide how you follow it and what you see along the way.

(Pause for 10 seconds.)

After the right amount of time, you might encounter a clearing where there are voices and songs and poetry and music and theater and comedy and so much more. The Muses are gathered for you. All of them have come together to delight in your name and in your willingness to meet with them.

Now, there are many Muses to meet, so you may not meet all of them and you may not hear from everyone. But this is just a first meeting of many. Know you can return again and again.

You might encounter Erato, Muse of Love Poetry. Or Calliope, Muse of Epic Poetry. Or Urania, Muse of Astronomy. Or Thalia, Muse of Comedy. Or Clio, Muse of History. Or Melpomene, Muse of Tragedy. Or Euterpe, Muse of Music. Or Terpsichore, Muse of Dance. Or Polyhymnia, Muse of Sacred Poetry.

Follow your heart, your inspiration, your internal compass and sit with the Muses. Take time to listen, to ask questions, to interact, and to do whatever you can called to do in this meeting. This is your time.

(Wait a few minutes. I find that 5 minutes feels very long sometimes, but other times 20 minutes seems too short. For this first trance, shorter can be easier.)

While we can't stay in these magickal spaces for long, we can return. Take a few moments to finish your interactions, maybe offer thanks or a gift, before you head back.

(Wait a minute.)

It is time to return and if you have not thanked the Muses, this is a good time for that. Find the path again and make your way easily and quickly, finding yourself where you began.

However you widened your awareness and dropped into wisdom, begin to bring that back to your head and to your body. You are coming back to your body and out of the trance space.

Return to your neck and shoulders and arms, back back.
Return to your creative heart, lungs, and ribs, back back.
Return to your digestion and solar plexus, back back.
Return to your pelvic bowl, back back.
Return to your thighs, knees, and calves, back back.
And back to your toes and feet, back back.

Open your eyes if needed. State your name out loud three times. Think about what you last ate or the last movie you saw. It can help to drink some water or have a small snack (protein is best!). You can also write in a journal about your experience or rest.

Here are some prompts for your journal:

> What answers did I receive?
> What does my body feel like right now?
> What emotions did I feel during the experience?
> How do I feel now?

Trance work is a great way to interact with a deity and be open to whatever happens. The more you practice this work, the more you can deepen the experience, ask questions, and form a strong foundation for an ongoing relationship.

Chapter 2

The Birth & Family of the Muses

They were born in Pieria to Memory, queen of the foothills of Eleutherae, in union with the father, the son of Kronos; oblivion of ills and respite from cares. Nine nights Zeus the resourceful lay with her, going up to her holy bed far away from the immortals. And when the time came, as the months passed away and the seasons turned about, and the long tale of days was completed, she bore nine daughters – all of one mind, their carefree hearts set on song – not far from the topmost peak of snowy Olympus. There they have their gleaming dancing-places and their fair mansions; and the Graces and Desire dwell beside them, in feasting. Lovely is the sound they produce from their mouths as they sing and celebrate the ordinances and the good ways of all the immortals, making delightful utterance. So then they went to Olympus, glorying in their beautiful voices, singing divinely. The dark earth rang round them as they sang, and from their dancing feet came a lovely estampie[2] *as they went to their father. He is king in heaven; his is the thunder and the smoking bolt, since he defeated his father Kronos by strength. He has appointed their ordinances to the immortals, well in each detail, and assigned them their privileges.*

This is what the Muses sang, who dwell in Olympus,
the nine daughters born of great Zeus,
Clio and Euterpe and Thaleia and Melpomene,
Terpsichore and Erato and Polyhymnia and Urania,
and Calliope, who is chief among them all.

Theogony, Hesiod, Pg 4-5, translated by M.L. West

The Muses, Mousai (*Μουσαι* or *Μοῦσαι*), or the Pierides are the goddesses of song, music, and dance, serving as inspiration for others in their creative process. As the daughters of Memory, the Muses had access to all the knowledge in history, which they imparted to others. While the Muses are often seen with distinct items (which we'll talk about soon), they started as youthful goddesses with musical instruments. And Burkert notes, "[T]he Muses sing with beautiful voices" (146).

According to *Theogony* and other sources, the Muses were born in Pieria at the base of Mount Olympus. However, they have also been associated with other birthplaces, as well as a myriad of potential parents. Of note is how Hesiod's description of the Muses includes "oblivion of ills and respite from cares," which has been noted to describe how these beings allowed people to forget their pain and stop attending to their obligations.[3] In some descriptions, the Muses focused only on their creativity, not human life and activities.

"[T]he Muses, the Nereides, and Oceanides are choruses of young girls" (Burkert 173), and celebrated in ancient Greek society, often invoked before poetry writing and in rituals.

The Parents of the Muses

They [The Muses] were born on Pieria after our Father
Cronion [Cronus]
Mingled with Memory [Mnemosyne], who rules
Eleutherai's hills.
She bore them to be a forgetting of troubles,
A pause in sorrow. For nine nights wise Zeus
Mingled with her in love, ascending her sacred bed
In isolation from other Immortals.,
But when the time drew near, and the seasons turned,
And the moons had waned, and the many days were
done,
She bore nine daughters, all of one mind, with song

In their breasts, with hearts that never failed,
Near the topmost peak of snowcapped Olympos.
Invocation to the Muses in Theogony, Hesiod,
translated by S. Lombardo

Like many deities and beings in Greek mythology, the stories are told in a few texts. Depending on the translations and the translators, the Muses have different sets of parents, including:

- Zeus and Mnemosyne – King of the Godds and Titan Goddess of Memory (source: *Theogony*)
- Zeus (sources: *The Odyssey, Homeric Hymns*)
- Mnemosyne (sources: fragments)
- Uranus and Gaia – Primordial godds of Sky and Earth (sources: fragments)[4]
- Uranus[5] (sources: fragments)[6]
- Harmonia[7] – Goddess of Harmony; daughter of Aphrodite and Ares (Pausanias' writings)
- Zeus and Plousia (a nymph) – Tzetzes' writings
- Apollo – godd of oracles, music, song, healing, and more – Tzetzes' writings
- Pieros (King of Emathia in Macedonia) and Antiope (Princess of Hyria) – John Tzetzes' writings, Cicero's *De Natura Deorum*

Some say the Muses are "the fruits of nine nights of love-making" (Grimal 281), while Apollodorus notes in *The Library of Greek Mythology* that "Zeus married Hera and fathered Hebe, Eileithuia, and Ares; but he had intercourse with many other women, both mortal and immortal....and by Mnemosyne the Muses, first Calliope, and then Cleio, Melpomene, Euterpe, Erato, Terpsichore, Ourania, Thaleia, and Polymnia" (Apollodorus 29-30). Other sources describe Mnemosyne as a young woman who was bewildered by Zeus.[8]

Other sources[9] note that the Muses may also have been formed from the stamping of Pegasus' feet, causing four springs to emerge on Mount Helicon, which birthed pegasides,[10] nymphs related to water and springs.

The godd Apollo is said to have been a close companion to the Muses, and some writings speak of him being a parental figure to the Muses after their birth. However, I cannot find clear source(s) for the claim of Apollo and Eufime, a nymph, raising the Muses when Mnemosyne gave her babies away.

Epithets & Titles for the Muses

Epithets are commonly found in Greek mythology to help expand the understanding of a deity or being. They are often used alongside the deity's name or on their own to help invoke a particular energy.

I was surprised by how few titles and epithets there are for the Muses (or reliable sources for them). For beings of inspiration, I thought there might be more poetic descriptions of and for them. Most epithets are related to places where the Muses have been said to have been celebrated or born.

- Pierides / Pierides / **Πιεριδες** – Of Pieria.
- Olympiades / Olympiades / **Ολυμπιαδες** – Of Olympus.
- Helikônides / Heliconides / **Ἑλικωνιδες** – Of Mount Helicon.
- Ilisiades / Ilisiades / **Ιλισιαδες** – Of Ilissos/Ilissus River.
- Parthenoi Helikôniai / Partheni Heliconiae / **Παρθενοι Ἑλικωνιαι** – Maidens of Helicon.
- Aganipídis / Aganippides[11] / **Αγανιπίδης** – Of a spring at the base of Mount Helicon.
- Castalides[12] / Kastalides / **Κασταλίδης** – Of a spring that the nymph Castalia either jumped into or transformed into when escaping Apollo.
- Libethrides[13] / Leibêthrides / **Λιβεθρίδης** – Of this favorite place of the Muses place was where they buried Orpheus.

- Pegasides[14] / Pigasídis / **Πηγασίδες** – Of the beloved Hippocrene spring.
- Pimple'is / Pimplea / **Πιμπληίς** – Of Mount Pimplias in Pieria.

These titles and epithets are used in invocations and hymns to the Muses. This is important to know because not only can you use these names in rituals and devotional work, but they can also be used to 'find' the Muses in pieces of writing. While the Muses can sometimes seem to be 'missing' from literature, they might be referred to by other names that were more common in certain areas and time periods.

Practice: Birthing Creativity

With all the possibilities in the number of Muses, it further offers the reminder that different perspectives yield different creative answers to the same question. There may not be one answer which is not only valid but also something that can invoke curiosity about what else may require exploration and contemplation.

I like to think of these thoughts from poets, writers, geographers, and scholars as ways the creativity of the Muses was also born into the world. When trying to understand the forces of inspiration, they were inspired to birth new ideas and conversations that continued for centuries.

In this practice, I offer a way to connect with the Muses to birth creativity for yourself, your community, or the sheer pleasure of being creative. This can help you if you have been stuck or just want a new perspective on a lingering question.

What you will need:

Paper, pen, or other writing utensil
Scissors

Your choice:

Markers, pens, or pencils
Art supplies
Collage materials
Musical instrument
Camera
Anything else that you associate with your creativity or the creativity you want to birth

One thing to keep in mind is that you can adapt this practice to your particular medium of creativity. Allow inspiration to inspire you, allow the Muses to whisper in your ear about new directions and unconsidered possibilities.

Start by thinking of a question about your creativity. This might be a question about a certain project, a certain obstacle, a lingering worry, etc.

Examples:

Why am I blocked right now?
What do I need to create?
How do I go ahead with this ________ project?
Is there something I'm missing about ________ project?

I encourage you to come up with a question that is open-ended and one that cannot be answered with 'yes' or 'no.' This question should be asking for a longer answer versus a quick response.

Once you have your question ready, take a few moments to ground yourself and become present in the moment. You may do this by taking a few deep breaths, tensing and relaxing your muscles, shaking out any tension, etc. When you feel focused on what is before you, it's wise to ask the Muses for their help and inspiration. You might call out their names or just call out to their wisdom and inspiration. Ask that they witness you and inform you. Ask that their unique talents offer you what you need.

When you begin to feel the Muses arrive or you feel they have been welcomed to join you, you can take a few paths:

> Write about the question as though the Muses were holding your hand. Write down any words that arrive in your mind, without thinking if they make sense or if they answer your question. Keep writing until you feel you have heard all the Muses have to offer.
>
> Draw a picture or sculpt or paint whatever you are moved to create as you ask the Muses the question again and again. This process doesn't have to make sense or be leading in any direction.

Or you can use another medium to create something in response to the question you have. Think about the question while you play your guitar or the piano. Think about your question as you take pictures or video yourself dancing. Think about your question as you record yourself singing a tune without any words. Drop into the possibilities for creativity. There is no goal here, just experience and immersion in the experience until you feel done.

Whenever you feel done, look at what you have created. Or watch it. Or listen to it again.

What emerged from the process? What has been born? When you think of your question again, what does this creative piece have to tell you? Does it have an answer? What might it be offering to you? If you're not sure, a way to look at the final piece is to describe it to yourself in fine detail, without adding any story or interpretation.

For example:

> *The blue painting has three different tones of blue in it. The strokes of the painting are wide in most places, but thinner in*

> *the right corner. There are no other colors, except for a small dot of black in the lower left corner. It's not a circle, but an oval with a space in the middle.*

Then you might think about what your mind and body felt like during the creation:

> *The feeling when I was painting felt like fear, but it also felt like the fear was from a long time ago. My mind felt unsure and worried that I wasn't going to do it right. My body felt shaky and as though I was younger than my current age.*

From there, you might go back to your question:

> *I wanted to know why I wasn't painting as much as I used to. It's something I enjoy, but every time I start, I tend to give up really quickly. When I think about the question and the painting, I can see that the blues I chose also feel sad and scared. There are places where it's really wide and big, and also a place where it's crushed and small. The dot seems like it is me, but really far away, trying to decide if I should go to the place with the thinner brush strokes because that place seems more exciting.*

Take a breath and ask the Muses if you need more clarification:

> *I need to get away from places that feel too big and scary to paint again. I can paint on my own or with a small group of friends. This can make things less scary.*

While you might not follow this script, notice how it moves in this way:

- What is happening?
- How does it feel?

- What might it mean?
- Is there more the Muses could offer?

When you feel complete, thank the Muses for their help and put the creation on an altar to them or in a place of reverence. You will then be reminded how you can birth and rebirth your creativity and that the answers to your questions can be divinely inspired.

Chapter 3

Who Are the Muses?

Men have given the Muses their name from the word muein, which signifies the teaching of those things which are noble and expedient and are not known by the uneducated.27 For the name of each Muse, they say, men have fond a reason appropriate to her: Cleio is so named because the praise which poets sing in their encomia bestows great glory (kleos) upon those who are praised; Euterpê, because she gives to those who hear her sing delight (terpein) in the blessings which education bestows; Thaleia, because men whose praises have been sung in poems flourish (thallein) through long periods of time; Melpomenê, from the chanting (melodia) by which she charms the souls of her listeners; Terpsichorê, because she delights (terpein) her disciples with the good things which come from education; Erato,28 because the makes those who are instructed by her men who are desired and worthy to be loved; Polymnia, because by her great (polle) praises (humnesis) she brings distinction to writers whose works have won for them immortal fame; Urania, because men who have been instructed of her she raises aloft to heaven (ouranos), for it is a fact that imagination and the power of thought lift men's souls to heavenly heights; Calliopê, because of her beautiful (kale) voice (ops), that is, by reason of the exceeding beauty of her language she winds the approbation of her auditors.

Diodorus Siculus, The Library of History,
Book IV, Chapter 7, lines 5 onward,
translated by Charles Henry Oldfather

Homer and Hesiod were thought to have a unique ability to see and describe the gods. According to Herodotus, those two poets 'first revealed to the Greeks how the gods were born, what they were called, which honors and powers they enjoyed, and how they looked.' This task, however, was far from straightforward (Graziosi 29).

One wondrous and potentially complicated part of the Muses is how they are represented in texts. Though the Muses are respected and honored, they also seem concerned about whether they should help someone like Hesiod in writing his epic poem, *Theogony*.

[Hesiod] knew that as an epic poet, he must begin with the Muses and ask them for information – but the Muses, daughters of Zeus and Memory, were relatively recent goddesses. He wanted to talk about a time before their time, a time even before Zeus's time, a time before the beginning of everything. Eventually, he compromised by offering several false beginnings (Graziosi 29-30).

In *Theogony,* Hesiod starts with an invocation to the Muses, one that precedes the description of the family tree, helping show the knowledge of the Muses extends far into the past. Then, Hesiod talks about how he met the Muses while tending sheep on Mount Helicon. The Muses were critical of his poetry and even more critical of shepherds.

One of my favorite writings about the Muses arrives in M.L. West's translation of *Theogony*: "Shepherds that camp in the wild, disgraces, merest bellies: we know to tell many lies that sound like truth, but we know to sing reality, when we will." But the Muses decide to tell Hesiod the truth, and this is why the next starting point of his poem is a more extended hymn to the Muses.

The idea that the Muses were conscious of whether they told the truth offers another way to look at the stories from ancient Greece. Does this description mean the stories are not to be trusted? Who is worthy of hearing the truth? Is Hesiod relaying the truth?

How Many Muses Are There?

The Muses were nine in number, the daughters of Zeus and Mnemosyne, Memory. At first, like the Graces, they were not distinguished from each other. "They are all," Hesiod says, "of one mind, their hearts are set upon song and their spirit is free from care. He is happy whom the Muses love. For though a man has sorrow and grief in his soul, yet when the servant of the Muses sings, at once he forgets his dark thoughts and remembers not his troubles. Such is the holy gift of the Muses to men."

Mythology, Edith Hamilton, Pg. 39-40

While we'll go into the specifics of the Muses, there has been some debate about how many Muses there are. Hesiod[15] names Clio ("Proclaimer"), Euterpe ("Well Pleasing"), Thaleia ("The Blooming" or "Luxuriant"), Melpomene ("Songstress"), Terpsichore ("Delighting in the Dance"), Erato ("Lovely"), Polyhymnia ("She of Many Hymns"), Urania ("Heavenly"), and Calliope ("She of the Beautiful Voice") as the Muses.

Bell writes:

> "Three Muses were worshipped also at Sicyon, but we have the name of only one of them, Polymatheia.[16] Again, three were worshipped at Delphi; their names corresponded with the names of the three strings of the lyre – Nete, Mese and Hypate. At Delphi they were alternately called Cephisso, Apollonis and Borysthenis."[17]

But Bell also points out that:,

> "Four Muses were at one time recognised – Thelxinoe, Aoede, Arche and Melete – two of the names having been used before. One of the persons associated with

> the Muses was Pierus. By some he was called the father of a total of seven Muses, called Neilo, Tritone, Asopo, Heptapora, Achelois, Tipoplo and Rhodia. At Athens, eight Muses were recognised before nine became the standard number."[18]

For me, the many possibilities for the Muses offer insight into how people of that time recognized the expansiveness of inspiration. There was a Muse to thank for every creative endeavor and outcome.

Here are more thoughts on the number of Muses:

> *But Kallipos (Callipus) of Korinthos in his History of Orkhomenos uses the verses of Hegesinos as evidence in support of his own views, and I too have done likewise, using the quotation of Kallipos himself...The sons of Aloeus held that the Mousai were three in number, and gave them the names of* ***Melete (Practice), Mneme (Memory)*** *and* ***Aoede (Song)****. But they say that afterwards Pieros (Pierus), a Makedonian (Macedonian), after whom the mountain in Makedonia was named.*
>
> Pausanias, Description of Greece 9.29.2 – 9.29.3, translated by W.H.S. Jones

There were also the Mousai Titanides:[19]

> *Again the first set of Musae (Muses) are* ***four****, the daughters of the second Jupiter [i.e. Ouranos (Uranus)],* ***Thelixonoe, Aode, Arche*** *and* ***Melete****. The second set are the offspring of the third Jupiter [i.e. Zeus] and Mnemosyne,* ***nine*** *in number.*
>
> Cicero, De Natura Deorum 3.21, translated by H. Rackham

> *We are told by Mnaseas that the Muses are the daughters of Tellus (Earth) [Gaia] and Coelus (Heaven) [Ouranos]; others declare that they are Jove's by his wife Moneta [Mnemosyne, Memory], or Mens (Mind); some relate that they were virgins, others that they were matrons. For now we wish to touch briefly on the points where you are shown, from the difference of your opinions, to make different statements about the same thing. Ephorus, then, says that they are* ***three*** *in number; Mnaseas, whom we mentioned, that they are* ***four****; Myrtilus brings forward* ***seven****; Crates asserts that there are* ***eight****; finally Hesiod, enriching heaven and the stars with gods, comes forward with* ***nine*** *names.*
>
> Arnobius, Against the Heathen 3.37

Tzetzes[20] named the nine Muses: Kallichore, Helike, Eunike, Thelxinoë, Terpsichore, Euterpe, Eukelade, Dia, and Enope.

With this information, we can see there are different numbers of Muses, different names of Muses, different thoughts on parentage, and more. However, as with many stories about mythology and studies of ancient beings, prominent voices often have the last word. And as for the 'traditional' number and names of the Muses, we have Hesiod and Homer (and others) to thank.

Original Boeotian Muses[21]

The history of writings about the Muses begins in Boeotia[22], while there are also three Thracian[23] Muses. Also known as the Elder Muses, the Boeotian Muses are the Muses that were said to be born of Gaia and Uranus.

- Aoede (Song)
- Melete (Practice or Meditation)[24]
- Mneme (Memory)[25]

Cicero also names Elder Muses in *De Natura Deorum*, including:

- Aoede
- Melete
- Arche (Beginning)
- Thelxinoe (Charming the Mind)

Olympian Muses

When most refer to the Muses, they are referencing the nine Olympian Muses: Calliope, Clio, Erato, Euterpe, Melpomene, Polyhymnia, Thalia, Terpsichore, and Urania, but earlier references speak of three Muses.[26]

The Olympian Muses could be considered the most well-known due to the popularity of Hesiod's and Homer's writings. These Muses continue to emerge in stories and are also found in art. While their names have different spellings, depending on translations, these are the nine Muses.

> "The Muses performed the same function on Olympus as the poets, writers and musicians that they inspired in the mortal world…They spent time regaling the main Olympians with stories of the exploits of both gods and men from across history, including tales of future events. Rarely, they also sang in front of mortals, such as at the wedding celebrations of the sea nymph Thetis and Peleus and the funerals of Patroclus and Achilles" (Roberts 156).

The Role of Apollo

In Claude Lorrain's (1674) drawing, *Apollo and the Muses*,[27] the Muses appear to be seated around Apollo, listening to him play a lyre. In other descriptions of Apollo in the Orphic Hymns, he is described as the 'Muses' head'[28] or the Mousagetos (Leader of the Muses).[29] These titles seem to indicate a relationship that may have been instructive or collaborative. Other writings indicate that Apollo may have been in love with all of the Muses, but he remained unmarried as he could not choose one. While other writings point to art as indicative of Apollo being a frequent companion to the Muses and someone who leads the Muses in dance.

In Plato's *Laws*,[30] he speaks of the Muses and Apollo being invited to feasts so that children who are undisciplined might associate feasts with these teachers and be inspired again.

The Muses Apollonides[31] (Mousai Apollônides) are said to be the daughters of Apollo. These muses were honored at Delphi, with one being called Kephiso (Cephiso) after the local river. The other three were Nete, Mese, and Hypate after the strings of the lyre, from lowest to highest respectively.

> *But Eumelos (Eumelus) of Korinthos (Corinth) says there are three Mousai (Muses), daughters of Apollon: Kephiso (Cephiso), Apollonis, and Borysthenis.*
>
> Eumelus, Fragment 35, translated by M. L. West

But as the connection between the Muses and Apollo is difficult to quantify, Ginette Paris offers this perspective, "Historians like to believe, and have us believe, that they're the best repositories of collective memory, the best guardians of culture.... They are after truth, not myth; facts, not fiction. They have forgotten that the Muses, sources of culture, were daughters of Mnemosyne before they were servants of Apollo" (Paris 133).

Calliope / Kalliope: Epic Poetry

> *[The Mousai (Muses) came to sing the dirge at the funeral of Akhilleus (Achilles):] To Thetis spake Calliope, she in whose heart was steadfast wisdom throned: 'From lamentation, Thetis, now forbear, and*

do not, in the frenzy of thy grief for thy lost son, provoke to wrath the Lord of Gods and men. Lo, even sons of Zeus, the Thunder-king, have perished, overborne by evil fate. Immortal though I be, mine own son Orpheus died, whose magic song drew all the forest-trees to follow him, and every craggy rock and river-stream, and blasts of winds shrill-piping stormy-breathed, and birds that dart through air on rushing wings. yet I endured mine heavy sorrow: Gods ought not with anguished grief to vex their souls. Therefore make end of sorrow-stricken wail for thy brave child; for to the sons of earth minstrels shall chant his glory and his might, by mine and by my sisters' inspiration, unto the end of time. Let not thy soul be crushed by dark grief, nor do thou lament like those frail mortal women. Know'st thou not that round all men which dwell upon the earth hovereth irresistible deadly Aisa (Aesa, Fate), who recks not even of the Gods? Such power she only hath for heritage. Yea, she soon shall destroy gold-wealthy Priamos' (Priam's) town, and Trojans many and Argives doom to death, whom so she will. No God can stay her hand.' So in her wisdom spake Calliope.

Quintus Smyrnaeus, Fall of Troy 3. 631 ff,
translated by A.S. Way

Calliope is known to be the leader (Chief of all Muses) and/or the Muse who was born first. Her name means 'Beautiful Voice' and is thought to be the mother of Orpheus (by Apollo or Thracian King Oeagrus) and Hymen and Ialemus (by Apollo). She might also be the mother of Rhesus, a Thracian king who died in the Trojan War, or Linus, who invented melody and rhythm.

Calliope is said to have inspired Homer's *The Odyssey* and *The Iliad*. She is often pictured with a writing tablet, book, or scroll. She wears a diadem, or a crown-like piece, in some imagery to note her role among the Muses.

Lovers: Apollo, Oeagrus, Zeus
Children: Orpheus, Linus, the Corybantes

Suggested Practices:

- Singing
- Writing poetry
- Reading epic poetry
- Leading others in singing or writing
- Listening to music

Clio / Cleio: History

For there was a shrine of the Mousai (Muses) here [south of Apollon's temple at Delphoi (Delphi)] where the spring wells up, and that is why they used this water for libation and lustrations, as Simonides says: 'where the holy water of the lovely-haired Moisai (Muses) is drawn from below for lustration. Overseer of the holy lustration-water, golden Kleio (Clio), who give the water-drawers from the ambrosial cave the fragrant lovely water sought with many prayers.'

Simonides, Fragment 577,
translated by David Campbell

While most descriptions of Clio speak of her relationship with history, it's better to say that she documents history and announces victories. In imagery, Clio holds a trumpet-like instrument for shouting accomplishments, or she holds a scroll for documenting what happens for historical reference. Clio also is seen with a water clock, or a clepsydra.[32]

As her name means 'glory,' this is why Clio is associated with recording heroic deeds and tales. She was also said to be the mother of Hyacinthus by Pierus, the king of Macedonia, as a result of criticizing Aphrodite for falling in love with Adonis. In retaliation for the criticism, Aphrodite punished Clio and made her fall in love with the king.

Lovers: Pierus
Children: Hymenaeus, Hyacinthus

Suggested Practices:

- Learning about the land you live on
- Reading about the history of conflict, and finding multiple sources of stories
- Writing a story of your personal heroism or others' heroism in your life
- Share your daily victories with others
- Posting good news on social media

Erato: Love Poetry and Lyric Poetry

From them the locust tribe afterwards arose, and they have this gift from the Muses, that from the time of their birth they need no sustenance, but sing continually, without food or drink, until they die, when they go to the Muses and report who honors each of them on earth. They tell Terpsichore of those who have honored her in dances, and make them dearer to her; they gain the favor of Erato for the poets of love, and that of the other Muses for their votaries, according to their various ways of honoring them; and to Calliope, the eldest of the Muses, and to Urania who is next to her, they make report of those who pass their lives in philosophy and

> *who worship these Muses who are most concerned with heaven and with thought divine and human and whose music is the sweetest. So for many reasons we ought to talk and not sleep in the noontime.*
>
> Plato, Phaedrus, line 259,
> translated by Harold N. Fowler

Erato is the muse of love poetry, lyric poetry, and erotic poetry. Her name is translated to 'desired' or 'lovely.' Strongly connected to Eros, Erato is often said to be the inspiration for stories of ill-fated lovers.

She is seen wearing a myrtle crown and holding a lyre and was seen with more love-related symbols (akin to Aphrodite) during the Renaissance. For example, Erato's later images included roses and doves.

Lovers: Malus
Children: Cleophema

Suggested Practices:

- Write love poems to yourself, to others, to the world
- Read love poetry aloud to yourself and others
- Write about love stories in your life, not just romantic ones
- Make a playlist of love songs
- Learn about the different kinds of love and where they have happened in your life

Euterpe: Double-Pipes and Music / Lyrical Poetry

> *To each of the Muses men assign her special aptitude for one of the branches of the liberal arts, such as poetry, song, pantomimic dancing, the round dance with music, the study of the stars, and the other liberal arts. They are*

> *also believed to be virgins, as most writers of myths say, because men consider that the high attainment which is reached through education is pure and uncontaminated. Men have given the Muses their name from the word muein, which signifies the teaching of those things which are noble and expedient and are not known by the uneducated. For the name of each Muse, they say, men have found a reason appropriate to hee...Euterpe, because she gives to those who hear her sing delight (terpein) in the blessings which education bestows*
>
> Diodorus Siculus, Library of History 4.7.3, translated by Charles Henry Oldfather

Euterpe is a Muse of lyrical poetry, music, and tragedy,[33] often pictured playing the aulos, the double flute. She developed many instruments and was described as using noise-makers. Like her sister Calliope, Euterpe was also said to possibly be the mother of Rhesus, the Thracian king who died in the Trojan War, according to a description in Apollodorus' *The Library of Greek Mythology*.

In a fresco found in Pompeii,[34] Euterpe is shown with a crown of laurel leaves on her head, in a blue and gold gown, playing a flute. There are also flutes placed around her.

Lovers: Apollo, Strymon
Children: Rhesus

Suggested Practices:

- Play music on an instrument, a flute if possible
- Try to speak up more often and use your voice in the world
- Write poems about delight
- Listen to the music of everyday sounds and noises
- Find double flute music and listen to it

Melpomene: Tragedy

[Ostensibly a description of an ancient Greek painting:] Why do you delay, O divine Sophocles, to accept the gifts of Melpomene? Why do you fix your eyes upon the ground? Since I for one do not know whether it is because you are now collecting your thoughts, or because you are awe-stricken at the presence of the goddess. But be of good heart, good sir, and accept her gifts; for the gifts of the gods are not to be rejected...Indeed you see how the bees fly above you, and how they buzz with a pleasant and divine sound as they anoint you with mystic drops of their own dew, since this more than anything else is to be infused into your poesy. Surely someone will before long cry out, naming you the "honeycomb of kindly Muses," and will exhort everyone to beware lest a bee fly unnoticed from your lips and insert its sting unawares. You can doubtless see the goddess herself imparting to you now sublimity of speech and loftiness of thought, and measuring out the gift with gracious smile.

Philostratus the Younger Imagines, Sophocles 13,
translated by Arthur Fairbanks

Known as the muse of the chorus and tragedy, Melpomene's name means 'to sing.' Imagery of her shows her holding a tragedy mask, the counterpart to Thalia's mask. According to many writers (Apollodorus, Lycophron, and Gaius Julius Hyginus), Melpomene was the mother of the Sirens, who would sing to passing ships and sailors to lure them to their death.

Melpomene is sometimes described as having a dagger and a cup, while she is more commonly shown with a laurel leaf or grapevine wreath around her head.

Lovers: Achelous
Children: Sirens

Suggested Practices:

- Write about a tragedy in your life and what you learned
- Give thanks for the gifts of tragedy
- Walk in nature to find examples of tragedy
- Sing to yourself about sad times in your life
- Create a playlist that captures the emotions of your life's disappointments

Polymnia/Polyhymnia: Hymns and Sacred Poetry

Declare to me, ye [the Mousai] who haunt the springs of Aganippian Hippocrene, those dear traces of the Medusaean steed. The goddesses disagreed; of them Polyhymnia began the first; the others were silent, and noted her saying in their mind. "After chaos, as soon as the three elements were given to the world, and the whole creation resolved itself into new species, the earth subsided by its own weight, and drew the seas after it, but the sky was borne to the highest regions of its own lightness; the sun, too, not checked by gravity, and the stars, and you, ye horses of the moon, ye bounded high."

Ovid, Fasti, Book V,
translated by James George Frazer

Polymnia or Polyhymnia is the muse of hymns and sacred poetry, and it's no surprise her name translates to 'one of many praises.' She is also associated with dance, agriculture, and pantomime.

Imagery of Polyhymnia often shows her veiled and putting a finger to her mouth, as though to keep the watcher from being too loud. Her face is often thoughtful and earnest. It's possible that Polyhymnia may also be the mother of Orpheus. She is also said to be a virgin in some writings, which connects her to how she is seen as sacred.

Lovers: Cheimarrhus, Celeus
Children: Orpheus, Triptolemus, Eros

Suggested Practices:

- Sit in silence
- Make a list of things to praise in your life
- Pay attention to the noises in the world and what surprises you
- Write a poem that celebrates what is sacred in your life
- Move your body in a dance without words to show your gratitude to her

Terpsichore / Terpsikhore: Dance

For in those days the Muse was not yet a lover of gain, nor did she work for hire. And sweet gentle-voiced odes did not go for sale, with silvered faces, from honey-voiced Terpsichore. But as things are now, she bids us heed [10] the saying of the Argive man, which comes closest to actual truth: "Money, money makes the man," he said, when he lost his wealth and his friends at the same time.

Pindar, Isthmian Ode 2. 6 ff,
translated by Diane Arnson Svarlien

As the muse of song and dance, Terpsichore's name is often translated to 'Delightful Dancing' or 'Delight in Dancing.' While she was well-known among the Muses, there were few stories about Terpsichore. Some writings indicate she may have been the mother of the Sirens (as opposed to Melpomene) or Linus.

Pictured with a lyre, Terpsichore is sometimes seen in art with feathers behind her ears.

Lovers: Apollo, Achelous, Ares
Children: Linus, Biston, Sirens

Suggested Practices:

- Dance, dance, dance
- Find a way to dance while being out in public
- Sing a song that reminds you of sweetness
- Watch performances of dance and song
- Try dancing with a tree or the ocean or another part of nature

Thalia / Thaleia: Comedy and Pastoral Poetry

If in Grecian dress he declaimed the Attic speech of fluent Menander [the writer of comedies], Thalia would have rejoiced and praised his accents, and in wanton mood have disordered his comely locks with a rosy garland.

Statius, Silvae 2. 1. 114 ff,
translated by J. H. Mozley

Known as the Muse of comedy, Thalia is a half of theater's comedy-tragedy masks with her sister Melpomene. Hesiod also names her as one of the Graces. As Apollo's lover, she may have mothered the Corybantes or the dancers who worshiped Cybele and muffled Zeus' cries when he was hidden away as a baby.

Thalia is pictured with a tragedy mask and sometimes with a shepherd's staff.

Lovers: Apollo
Children: Corybantes

Suggested Practices:

- Watch comedy shows and movies
- Seek out ways to bring humor to others
- Try listening to comedy that you would not have listened to before
- Write about funny times in your life or the people who have made you laugh the hardest
- Take a picture of yourself when you are laughing

Urania / Ourania: Astronomy & Astrology

Since fine-throned Ourania (Urania) has sent me from Pieria a golden cargo-boat laden with glorious songs.

Bacchylides, Fragment 16, translated by Sir Richard C. Jebb

Urania is the muse of astronomy and astrology, and her name means 'heavenly.' She is sometimes said to be the eldest muse, linking her to universal love. During the Renaissance, Urania was considered the muse for Christian poets.

Often holding a globe and a compass, Urania is not to be confused with Aphrodite Urania. Some records state that Urania may have been the mother of Linus or Hermes. She wears a cloak embroidered with stars as she looks up to the skies. Urania is said to be able to see the future in the stars.

Lovers: Apollo, Hermes, Amphimarus
Children: Linus, Hymen

Suggested Practices:

- Create your birth chart, or look at your birth chart again
- Take time to consider how astrology impacts you (or not)
- Read your horoscopes for a week and follow their wisdom

- Spend time looking up at the stars
- Consider how you relate to divine love and if you have experienced it

Images of the Muses

While these descriptions seem the most common and repeated in writings, the Muses also arrived in Rome. The author of the epic poem *Annales*, Ennius, wrote about the history of the Roman Republic and how the godds favored some men. In this poem, Ennius speaks of 'the Muses who dance on Olympus.' At the same time, Andronicus' translation of the *Odyssey* used a different name for the Muses: Camenae, a name used for Italian goddesses of fountains. However, Ennius did not appreciate this new name and noted that the Muses were Greek; thus, the Romans needed to learn their Greek names (Graziosi 135).

In the Italian novel,[35] *Hypnerotomachia,* the book was filled with detailed illustrations integrated into the text. One of the buildings in the story is the (imaginary) Temple of Venus Physizoa, which includes internal columns with statues of Apollo and the Muses. The book includes sections on Apollo, Clio, Euterpe, Melpomene, Talia, Polimnia, Erato, Terpsicore, Urania, and Caliope. In the images, the Muses are shown with instruments, except for Urania who holds a compass and Clio who is riding a swan. Some of the Muses have orbs, while some do not.

There are also descriptions of the mother of Muses, Mnemosyne, with Lethe, the river of oblivion, one of five rivers in the underworld of Greek mythology.

> *For Mnemosyne and Lethe in Greek religion we are not however dependent on the myths and philosophy of Plato. We have definitive evidence in local ritual. Mnemosyne herself takes us straight to the North, the land of Eumolpos and the Muses, to Pangaion, to Pieria, to Helicon. If Orpheus found in*

> *Egypt, or as is more probable in Crete, a well of living water, that well was I think nameless, or at least did not bear the name of Mnemosyne. It may of course be accidental, but in the tablet from Crete the well, though obviously the same as that in the Petelia tablet, is unnamed. The name Mnemosyne was found for the well when Orpheus took it with him to the land of the Muses, where he himself got his magical lyre.* (Harrison 578)

Exercise: Choosing a Muse

According to Goodrich, the Muses were the ones who taught the first Delphic Oracle (306), which is something to keep in mind with this exercise. The Muses might have things to show you and tell you, perhaps acting as oracles for your questions about creativity and growth.

While you can work with the Muses as a group, you might be open to seeing if a particular Muse might have something to offer you right now. Here is a practice that can help you sink into the magick of each Muse to see which one is calling to you more than another.

To follow this practice, you will need:

- An item or a picture that represents each Muse
  - e.g., a book of love poems for Erato, a tragedy mask for Melpomene, etc. You can be creative and choose things you own instead of buying new items
- Journal and writing utensil

While creating a complicated or detailed ritual might be something you choose to do, this can also be a simple modern practice.

You'll want to start with finding a space where you will not be disturbed. You can cleanse before you start, ground, and create sacred space too. Ideally, you want to begin with a prayer or invocation to the Muses, asking for their wisdom and guidance. When working with a group of deities, I often tell them exactly what the ritual intends. In this case, you are opening to the wisdom of each of the Muses to see if one (or more) might want to work with you right now.

When you feel settled and present, you pick up an item and name it the Muse it represents. You can close your eyes and think about the Muse, allowing the energy of that Muse to fill the item and then travel up your arm into your mind and heart.

What do you feel? Or see? Or notice?
What do you learn?
Is there a message?

You can spend as much time as you like. When you feel ready to stop, imagine the energy moving back out of your body and into the item. Put the item down and away from your body. Write down anything you gleaned from the experience.

Repeat this process with each Muse.

If you notice one Muse is louder than the others, you may want to stop there. Or you can choose to continue with each item. You might also choose to have the same item for each Muse, perhaps with a label for their name, so you don't know who you are tapping into when you invite their energy into your body.

Either way will work, and it might be wise to try both ways to experience them.

Please know you don't have to visualize things in your mind for this to work. All you need to do is to open to the energy of each Muse and notice what you notice. There is no ideal way to do this, nor are there certain ways the Muses interact. Your experience will be unique and suitable for your energy. I would just encourage you to focus on staying curious about what you notice and sense, without judgment or expectation.

Sometimes the clearest answers are the ones you don't realize are trying to tell you something.

This practice can be repeated whenever you like, and it can be adapted to just be for one Muse at a time, in case you want to sink more deeply into one energy over another.

Chapter 4

Stories & Myths of the Muses

[At the wedding of Cadmus and Harmonia:] The nine Muses too struck up a life stirring melody: Polymnia nursing mother of the dance waved her arms, and sketched in the air an image of a soundless voice, speaking with hands and moving eyes in a graphic picture of silence full of meaning.

Nonnus, Dionysiaca 5. 88 ff,
translated by William Henry Denham Rouse

In Greek myths, the Muses seem to have a function more than they have distinct personalities or stories. While they are mentioned in some interactions, they are not the focal point, nor does a reader understand their individuality. They are often pictured together or described in broad terms, leaving them somewhat challenging to discern.

Not to veer too far away from the Greek pantheon, but I've noticed this too in the stories (or lack thereof) of the Norns in the Norse pantheon. These beings were central to time and fate but weren't very present in stories. Perhaps this relates to how beings like Hestia and Iris also show up – in everyday life and integral moments. They are in many places, but not the main characters. And yet, if they weren't present, the stories would be different.

When the Muses are the inspiration for stories and the retellers of stories, what stories are told of them? How do those who inspire the writing of stories become a part of the narrative? Or is it like the person who always takes pictures is the one who is never in the photos?

The Anger of the Muses

While the Muses are often contemplated for the gifts of their inspiration and their willingness (eventually) to give information to poets, their anger is often missed. But writers and poets described several moments when the Muses displayed their capability for wrath.

Thamyris

> *Dorion, where the Muses encountered Thamyris the Thracian stopped him from singing as he came from Oichalia and Oichalian Eurytos; for he boasted that he would prevail, if the very Muses, daughters of Zeus who holds the aegis, were singing against him, and these in their anger struck him maimed, and the voice of wonder they took away, and made him a singer without memory.*
>
> Homer, Iliad 2. 594 ff,
> translated by Richmond Lattimore

When Thamyris realized he was in love with Hyacinthus/ Hyacinth, which is noted as being the first time a male fell in love with a male,[36] he decided to use his talent for singing to sway Apollo into granting that love. As those songs failed, Thamyris decided to challenge the Muses to a contest, and lost, leaving him without a voice and gouging his eyes out.

The Sirens

> *A little lower down is a sanctuary of Hera with an ancient image, the work of Pythodorus of Thebes; in her hand she carries Sirens. For the story goes that the daughters of Achelous were persuaded by Hera to compete with the Muses in singing. The Muses won, plucked out the Sirens' feathers (so they say and made crowns for themselves out of them.*
>
> Pausanias, Description of Greece, 9. 34. 3,
> translated by W.H.S. Jones

Hera, queen of the godds and wife of Zeus, encouraged the Sirens, created with bodies of birds and heads of humans, to participate in a singing contest against the Muses. When the Sirens lost, and the Muses were victorious, the Muses plucked the feathers out of all the Sirens and made the feathers into crowns. The Sirens are said to have turned white and fallen into the sea, where they became islands. This battle was also shown in a third-century Roman sarcophagus.

Pyreneus

> *Pallas [Athena], having looked in wonder, for a long time, at this stream, made by the blow of the horse's hoof, gazed around her at the groves of ancient trees, the caves, and the grass, embroidered with innumerable flowers, and said that the daughters of Mnemosyne were equally happy in their home and their pursuits. At which one of the sisters answered, '...Our life is happy, if only it were safe. But (nothing is sacred to the wicked), all things frighten virgin minds. Dread Pyreneus's destruction is in front of my eyes, and my mind has not yet recovered fully. That fierce man had captured Daulis and the Phocian fields, with his Thracian warriors, and wrongly held the kingdom. We were heading for the shrine on Parnassus. He saw us going by, and his face showing apparent reverence for our divinity, he said (knowing us), "Mnemonides, wait, don't be afraid, I beg you, to shelter from the rain and the lowering skies" (it was raining): "The gods have often entered humbler homes". Responding to his words, and the weather, we gave the man our assent, and went into the entrance hall of the palace. The rain stopped, the north wind overcame the south, and the dark clouds fled from the clearing sky. We wished to go. Pyreneus closed the doors, and prepared for violence, and we escaped that only by*

taking to our wings. He stood on the highest summit, as if he would follow us, saying "Whatever is your way, is also mine", and foolishly threw himself from the roof of the main tower. He fell headlong, breaking his skull, hammering the ground in dying, and staining the earth with his evil blood.

Ovid, Metamorphoses 5, translated by A.S. Kline

The Muses go to Athena to tell them of their worry about Pyreneus, a king of Thrace. They speak of being afraid of the savagery of his actions, even though he said kind words and asked them to stay in his shelter out of the rain. But the king locked the Muses in the hall and would not let them leave. To escape, the Muses decide to fly away, which Pyreneus says he will also do to follow them. But in his hubris, he tries to fly out of a tower, only to fall to the ground, smashing his head into pieces.

The Muses & Death

Achilles' Funeral

The old Sea King's daughters gathered around you weeping, and they dressed you in clothes of the immortals. All nine Muses sang lamentations in their lovely voices. No one could keep from crying at the sound, so moving was their song. The gods and men were mourning seventeen long nights and days and then we gave you the pyre, and killed many fat sheep and cattle for your corpse. You burned in clothes from gods; you were anointed with oil and honey.

Homer, The Odyssey 24. 58 ff,
translated by Emily Wilson

The Muses sang a dirge at the funeral of Achilles, a song so deep that everyone wept as the song continued. Over seventeen days of mourning, the great Achilles was celebrated until his body was burned.

The Muses' Sons' Funerals

There are lays of paeans, coming in due season, which belong to the children of Leto of the golden distaff. There are other lays, which, from amid the crowns of flourishing ivy, long for the dithyramb of Dionysus; but in another song for did three goddesses lull to rest the bodies of their sons. The first of these sang a dirge over the clear-voiced Linus; and the second lamented with her latest strains Hymenaeus, who was seized by Fate, when first he lay with another in wedlock; while the third sorrowed over Ialemus, when his strength was stayed by the onset of a raging malady. But the son of Oeagrus, Orpheus of the golden sword... [fragment cuts off here]

Pindar, Dirges Fragment 139,
translated by Sir John Sandys

It is easy to forget that the Muses were also mothers, according to some writings. In this fragment, we see Terpsichore sing a dirge over Linus, Urania sing over Hymen, and Calliope sing over Ialmenus. The final sentence seems like it might be speaking of who mourned and lamented Orpheus, but the document I have showed no other words to complete the thought.

The Muses & Judgment

The Contest of Apollo and Marsyas

Marsyas, a shepherd, son of Oiagrus, one of the satyrs, found them, and by practicing assiduously kept making sweeter sounds day by day, so that he challenged Apollo to play the lure in a contest with him. When Apollo came there, they took the Muses as judges. Marsyas was departing as victor, when Apollo turned his lyre upside down, and played the same tune – a thing which Marsyas couldn't do with the pipes. And so Apollo defeated Marsyas, bound him to a tree, and turned him over to a Scythian who stripped his skin off him limb by limb.

Hyginus, Fabulae 165, translated by Mary Grant

The anger of the Muses is already established, but they were also called on as judges of contests. In this contest between Apollo and Marsyas, Marsyas was certain he could outperform Apollo on his pipes, but Apollo turned the lyre upside down and played the same tune. Apollo was deemed the winner, and Marsyas was bound and killed in a gruesome manner.

The Muses & the Lyre

Hermes and the Muses

The clever device of the lyre, it is said, was invented by Hermes, who constructed it of two horns and a crossbar and a tortoise-shell; and he presented it first to Apollo and the Muses, then to Amphion of Thebes.

Philostratus the Elder, Imagines 1. 10.1,
translated by Arthur Fairbanks

Shortly after his birth at dawn, Hermes invented the lyre that afternoon by taking two horns, a crossbar, and a tortoiseshell (which he found upon running into the tortoise and killing it). According to some stories, Hermes presented the lyre to Apollo and the Muses.

More Muses Stories

Sphinx

For Hera sent the Sphinx, whose mother was Echidna and her father Typhon; and she had the face of a woman, the breast and feet and tail of a lion, and the wings of a bird. And having learned a riddle from the Muses, she sat on Mount Phicium, and propounded it to the Thebans.

Apollodorus, The Library of Greek Mythology, 3.5.8, translated by Sir James George Frazer

It is said that the Muses taught the Sphinx[37] the riddle that this monstrous creature used to test every traveler: ***What is it that has one voice and yet becomes four-footed and two-footed and three-footed?*** When the travelers did not guess correctly, the Sphinx would eat them. When Oedipus gave the right answer, the Sphinx killed itself.

Eros & Psyche's Wedding

Presently a rich wedding feast appeared. The bridegroom reclined at the head, clasping Psyche in his arms. Jupiter [Zeus] and Juno [Hera] sat beside them, and all the deities in order. Ganymede, the cup-bearing shepherd lad, served Jupiter his nectar, that wine of the gods, and Bacchus-Liber served all the rest, while Vulcan cooked the meal. Now the Hours [Horae] adorned everyone with roses and hosts of other flowers; the Graces scattered balsam; the choir of the Muses sounded; Apollo sang to the lyre, and Venus [Aphrodite] danced charmingly to that outpouring of sweet music, arranging the scene so the Muses chimed together, with a Satyr fluting away, and a woodland creature of Pan's piping his reeds. So Psyche was given in marriage to Cupid [Eros] according to the rite, and when her term was due a daughter was born to them both, whom we call Pleasure.'

Apuleius, The Golden Ass 6. 24 ff,
translated by A.S. Kline

The Muses were present at the marriage celebration of Psyche and Eros, at the request of Aphrodite. They sang while Apollo played the lyre, a satyr played a flute, Pan sang to the pipes, and Aphrodite danced.

The Muses and Artemis

[Artemis] goes to the great house of her dear brother Phoibos Apollon (Phoebus Apollo), to the rich land of Delphoi (Delphi), there to order the lovely dance of the Mousai (Muses) and Kharites (Charites, Graces). There she hangs up her curved bow and her arrows, and heads and leads the dances, gracefully arrayed, while all they utter their heavenly voice, singing.

Homeric Hymn 27 to Artemis 14 ff,
translated by Hugh G. Evelyn-White

Artemis is often seen in stories with her twin brother Apollo, and in this story, she asks for the Muses to dance while she is visiting her brother's house. The great hunter puts her bow to the side and leads the Muses and Graces in dances while singing together.

Practice: Stepping into Stories

When I want to get to know a deity (or more than one deity) better, I try to read as many stories as I can find about them. While the stories might be contradictory or told through the translator's lens, there is value in looking at how a deity is portrayed. For example, there aren't a lot of stories about the Muses, as you have seen. However, if you step into those stories with your imagination, you can learn more about the Muses and how they may have been perceived.

A practice of mine is to read a story, act the story out in my mind or within a group. Each person takes on the role of a character and then switches to play a new character. In doing so, you get a new perspective on the story and on the motivations and feelings of each being.

But since there are fewer stories about the Muses, I want to offer a slightly different practice.

In my training as a witch in the Reclaiming Witchcraft tradition, we learn and work with a practice inspired by Theatre of the Oppressed,[38] which was developed in the 1970s by Augusto Boal, a Brazilian theatre practitioner. In this practice, people take on different roles so that there is less distance between the audience and the actor.

When I have been in classes, this practice looked like someone telling a story and being a director and others being the story's actors. The actors learn about the story and act it out with the director's notes and guidance. Sometimes, the director can freeze the scene and change people into new roles or positions. Or the director can ask the actors to continue the story beyond what they were told, trusting their instincts and intuition.

So, one might get a group together to act as the Muses at the wedding of Psyche and Eros. The director might tell the actors what is happening and then say 'Action!' to start the play. When the play has used the information from the text, the director might say 'Cut!' and then tell the actors they will continue the wedding as the Muses or other characters to see what might unfold naturally.

While this is a retelling of the story, this practice also relies on trust and inspiration, which the Muses offer. See what happens when you don't stick so closely to a script. What might the Muses do or say? Discuss what happened and what inspiration may have come from the Muses themselves.

Chapter 5

Cults of the Muses

> Because the Muses have taught him, the poet can give instructions about every aspect of human life. A man should not pour a libation to Zeus and the other gods in the morning with unwashed hands, "for they do not hear you, and spit out your prayers." He should know what days of the month Zeus favors: the first, fourth, seventh, eighth, and ninth days are holy; the seventh was the day on which Zeus's son Apollo was born. (Lefkowitz 28)

First, it is important to know, or remember, that cults in ancient Greece are not the cults you see on various documentaries or shows. Instead, these cults are groups devoted to the practice of worshiping a deity. Sometimes, these cults were Mystery Cults, as in the cults of Dionysus and the cults of Demeter and Persephone. Since they were mysteries, there was little written about their practices. However, when we look at the Muses, we can see several cults across Greece, as evidenced by the remaining images.

The Many Cults of the Muses

The cults of the Muses were spread across Greece, with references by poets, writers, and travelers. For example, Cicero speaks in *De Natura Deorum*[39] of how Pythagoras would sacrifice an ox to the Muses whenever he came up with a new geometry discovery. In Greek Lyric V,[40] a line describes how Apollo and the Muses share a shrine or altar space.

Because Mount Helicon was a potential birthplace of the Muses, it is understandable this was a place of worship. Hesiod speaks of this at the very beginning of *Theogony:*

> *From the Muses of Helicon, let us begin our singing, that haunt Helicon's great and holy mountain, and dance on their soft feet round the violet-dark spring and the altar of the mighty son of Kronos. And when they have bathed their gentle skin in Permessos, or the Horse's fountain, or holy Olmeios, then on the highest slope of Helicon they make their dances, fair and lovely, stepping lively in time.*
>
> Theogony, Hesiod, Pg 1, translated by M.L. West

Strabo describes something similar:

> *Now Helicon, not far distant from Parnassus, rivals it both in height and in circuit; for both are rocky and covered with snow, and their circuit comprises no large extent of territory.5 Here are the temple of the Muses and Hippu-crene6 and the cave of the nymphs called the Leibethrides; and from this fact one might infer that those who consecrated Helicon to the Muses were Thracians, the same who dedicated Pieris and Leibethrum and Pimpleia to the same goddesses.7 The Thracians used to be called Pieres, but, now that they have disappeared, the Macedonians hold these places.*
>
> Strabo, Geography 9. 2. 25, edited by H.L. Jones

Pausanias' *Description of Greece* lets the reader know more about cults to the Muses. For example, the first to make sacrifices to the Muses on Mount Helicon were the Ephiates and Otos, who founded the village where Hesiod lived. Pausanias goes on to share that the sons of Aloeus noted there were three Muses named Melete (Practice), Mneme (Memory), and Aeode (Song). But then the Macedonian, Pieros, said there were nine Muses and changed their names to how they are now known as Olympian Muses. It should also be noted that Pieros may have had nine daughters with the same names.

Pausanias' writing describes a grove of the Muses on the left as one traveled down Mount Helicon. There, he said, you could see a portrait of Eupheme carved in stone, who was said to be the nurse of the Muses. Interestingly, there is a sculpture of Linos (Linus) that is said to receive sacrifices before the Muses, as he was killed by Apollo for being his singing rival, and people around the world visited to mourn his death.

> *The first images of the Muses are of them all, from the hand of Cephisodotus, while a little farther on are three, also from the hand of Cephisodotus, and three more by Strongylion, an excellent artist of oxen and horses. The remaining three were made by Olympiosthenes. There is also on Helicon a bronze Apollo fighting with Hermes for the lyre. There is also a Dionysus by Lysippus; the standing image, however, of Dionysus, that Sulla dedicated, is the most noteworthy of the works of Myron after the Erechtheus at Athens. What he dedicated was not his own; he took it away from the Minyae of Orchomenus. This is an illustration of the Greek proverb, "to worship the gods with other people's incense."*
>
> *Of poets or famous musicians they have set up likenesses of the following. There is Thamyris himself, when already blind, with a broken lyre in his hand, and Arion of Methymna upon a dolphin. The sculptor who made the statue of Sacadas of Argos, not understanding the prelude of Pindar about him, has made the flute-player with a body no bigger than his flute.*
>
> *Hesiod too sits holding a harp upon his knees, a thing not at all appropriate for Hesiod to carry, for his own verses make it clear that he sang holding a laurel wand.*
>
> Pausanias, Description of Greece 9. 30. 1 - 3,
> translated by W.H.S. Jones

Burkert describes the way the Muses dance around Apollo, but also wants a reader to know:

> A number of these groups exist only in myth, such as Titans and Gigantes. Others enjoy important cults, such as the Muses of Helicon, the Charities of Orchomenos, and the Kabeiroi. The existence of corresponding human cult associates cannot be proved in every case. In certain cases a normal type of cult may have replaced the earlier masked society; but only a fraction of the actual costumes ever found their way into our source material (174).

Remember again that mystery cults often remained mysterious, and the interpretations of what is known may have been impacted by those who completed the translations and research.

Southern Greece

Arcadia – According to Pausanias, there were images of the Muses, Hera, and Apollo before a sanctuary to Aphrodite in Megalopolis, as well as images of the Muses and Mnemosyne at a sanctuary to Athena in Tegea.

Argolis – There is a temple to the Muses in Troezen, built by the son of Hephaestus. Pausanias describes this as being a place where people made sacrifices to the Muses and Hypnos, as Hypnos was dearest to the Muses.

Attica – In Athens, Pausanias speaks of a shrine to Dionysus which included images of the Muses, Zeus, Athena, and Mnemosyne. Hermes and the Muses shared an altar at a school in outside of the city.

Corinth – A pedestal to Aphrodite in the marketplace in Corinth also included a relief to the Muses.

Elis – Between altars to the Graces and Dionysus, there is an altar to the Muses.

Lacedaemonia – In Sparta, there was a sanctuary to the Muses as the soldiers liked to enter battle by the sound of a flute with a harp accompanying it instead of a trumpet.

Central Greece

Boeotia – At a marketplace in Thespiae, there is a small bronze image of the goddess Nike and a small temple for the Muses.

Phocis – Pausanias describes shrines in Delphi to Apollo as including images of Apollo, Artemis, Leto, Helios, and the Muses.

Northern Greece

Macedonia – Here,[41] the Thracians, once called Pieres, left and then Macedonians emerged and continued to honor the Muses as peoples before did.

Muses & Festivals

Museia was a festival held every four[42] or five years[43], with one being held in the lower parts of Mount Helicon. There was also a celebration of the same name held at schools. The most detailed description I could find was about the Valley of the Muses.[44]

> The history of the famous Valley of the Muses on the eastern slopes of Mt. Helikon began in the 6th c. B.C. Its floruit period began from the 3rd c. B.C. onwards because of the 'Mouseia', festivals established and organised every 5 years by the Thespians. Poets and musicians from all over Greece also participated in various games (epic, poetry, rapsodia, kithara, aulos, satyric poetry, tragedy and comedy). In the 2nd and 1st c. B.C. were also added

> in the list game in honour of the roman emperor who from that time sponsored the whole organisation. The festivals were called onwards 'Great Kaisareia' because the emperor was honored at first place and not the Muses. The winners dedicated their tripods to the sanctuary. Hesiod did the same after his victory in Chalkis. Many statues depicting the Muses, famous poets and musicians stood in the open-air space of the Valley.[45]

Some sources note the celebration used to be an annual festival, with poets and musicians coming from all parts of Greece to compete. As the Romans took over, the emperors were then honored more than the Muses and winners of the festivals were carved into statues alongside statues to the Muses. And when monotheism spread, the festivals and the Valley of the Muses were abandoned.

Practice: Celebrating the Muses

Celebrating or acknowledging inspiration seems complicated today. There are articles about how inspiration isn't real or good for society. And there are articles about losing inspiration and how it's important to find it again. I've also seen articles critiquing those who attempt to be inspirational to others, even if their advice is dangerous.

In my eyes, this conversation about inspiration is intertwined with shame, capitalism, tall poppy syndrome, and Western culture's commitment to being 'self-made.' One can't claim to be inspired as it means they aren't enough alone. Or if they aren't making money from their inspiration or inspiring others, it's not 'real.' Or a person can't be 'too' inspirational, lest they show themselves to be bigger (taller) than others and thus think too highly of themselves. Or if someone just 'gets' an idea, then they aren't really doing things on their own. (Insert expletives and exasperation from me.)

The Muses are not beings that set out to be honored. They were birthed into the world because they are needed for culture to grow, innovate, and evolve. While there is a modern push for stories that show someone starting from nothing and figuring it out on their own, there are few (very few) stories that didn't include someone or something that helped along the way. Whether it was a kind word or a financial resource, those success stories had help.

And while there are many debates to be had about whether someone can be inspirational if they were helped 'too much' along the way, e.g., nepotism, generational wealth, etc., here's what I think is true. Inspiration exists regardless. Whether we recognize it is another conversation. Whether we want to share the credit with it is a larger discussion.

With all that said (steps off soapbox), celebrating inspiration is wise and worthwhile. My personal practice is that of celebrating what is offered to me, what is gifted to me, and what I have asked for. I also think celebrating with others is how we can begin to not only reduce any shame around our ideas and sharing them, but also how we can see how inspiration shows up for others – which might widen our own ability to recognize the Muses.

My invitation here is to gather some friends who want to create together. Everyone can create something different and bring along the tools and toys of their creation. Maybe you can gather outside or in a large room with the art supplies, the musical instruments, the unused notebooks and special journals, the baking ingredients, etc.

Together, you might stop and ask the Muses to grant you their inspiration and to offer you their witness during this time. Maybe you gift them with some small offerings and then you share time to create whatever arrives or you might work on things you feel stuck on. When you have this time together, you have this time to deepen into the energy of willingness to open to inspiration. And while you may not create the next bestseller or the newest five-star restaurant, creation is still worthy of time and energy.

When it's time to leave, I encourage you to go around the group and ask each person to share what they have created. This might include how they got the idea, what they did, and what surprised them. As each person shares, take care to listen deeply and celebrate them at the end. You can make noise, clap, toast to them, etc. And when everyone has shared, you might find some uplifting music and dance together, sing (even badly!) together, and enjoy this moment where inspiration has flowed in the room or space. Thank the Muses.

(Extra credit: share your creation publicly on social media or with a friend over a text message or the next time someone comes over to your space. Inspiration shared is inspiration offered.)

Chapter 6

Calling to the Muses for Help with Creativity

The number of guests at dinner should not be less than the number of the Graces nor exceed that of the Muses, i.e., it should begin with three and stop at nine.

Marcus Terentius Varro

So far, I have been blessed with more times of too many ideas than too few. But when I have had those moments when I need to create a blog or a song for a ritual, and inspiration isn't there, I can feel frustrated and worthless. Though I have come to know that these periods will pass, calling on the Muses has helped me find my way again.

I also find that the stronger a relationship I cultivate with the Muses, the less I need to turn to them. I trust in their support, and they see I act on their ideas. This is a symbiotic and reciprocal relationship that honors everyone by leading to more art and beauty in the world.

If you've skipped ahead to this chapter, I don't blame you. Being in the dark about what to do next or what to create is uncomfortable and liminal. While this chapter will certainly help you access the well of creativity again, it will also help to celebrate these goddesses on a more day-to-day basis, especially if you consider yourself creative. (And, in my eyes, everyone can call themselves that.)

> In Homer, knowledge is primarily visual. Humans are limited because they can only see so much. If they are to have extensive knowledge of the world, they need the gods or the muses, whose experience is wider.... In Greek

> philosophy the notion of the divine shifted from the existential immediacy and living images of myth to the realm of thoughts and abstract ideas...But notice what is significant here. The philosophers did not simply turn to thought alone; they presented thought as something divine (Hatab 164-165).

Do the Muses Meet You or Do You Meet Them?

Like the question of the chicken or the egg (which came first), the birth of inspiration can also seem confusing. Do the Muses come to you, or do you reach out to the Muses? In a previous chapter, I talked about my experience of the Muses often coming to me. And I think I know why this happens; at least, I think I have an idea.

I've been writing for many decades, sometimes in school, sometimes for work, and often for my enjoyment. It is probably true that I create something every single day, even if it's not writing. If I'm not working on a book, I'm taking pictures of nature. If I'm not taking pictures of nature, I'm writing a poem. If I'm not writing a poem, I sing made-up songs to my cats. If I'm not singing to my cats, I'm creating a ritual or a class plan. You get the idea.

What I think is true is that the Muses notice you more if you're already acting on your creative impulses. Just as Greek godds are said to be more interested in those who might worship them well, I think the same idea can be applied to these beings. When you are doing the work and you can be trusted to do the work that is creativity, they show up when you most need them.

Now, I also think the Muses can be called upon when you're stuck. After all, this does happen, and it happens even more frequently in a world where you are exposed to so many voices. It's not that you don't have another idea, but the noise of the world might cause you to think you don't have something new to say. In these situations, I would call on the Muses to support me in the best direction forward.

Here's what I would do if I felt creatively blocked:

Consider what I am doing – If I already knew about the Muses, and even if I didn't, I would stop and think about what action I was already taking. It might be that I'm not exposing myself to new ideas or places or that I'm just not sitting down at the place where I create. I would try to switch this up first and take the smallest step to see if that could create momentum.

Get quiet – When I feel overwhelmed by the push to create, I step back from the internet. I move away from all the voices and perspectives and inadvertent pressure to be unique and existing. If I am struggling, I might just need to go to the ocean or to the trees to settle my mind and detach from unnecessary expectations.

Ask for a sign – While this isn't necessarily a practice devoted to the Muses, if they are inspiration, then I might ask for a sign from them about the path to take. In most cases, this might not make a lot of sense, and it might not be the thing I need to do but recognizing there are signs can help me relax and know the Muses are there and watching.

Releasing ritual – When there is a blockage in my life, I often turn to a ritual of unbinding or cord-cutting. The simplest ritual I do is to use my athame to 'cut' away any unnecessary energetic cords around my body. I tell myself that I am removing anything that is standing in the way of the creative work I want to do. It always makes me feel better.

Once I have tried some or all of the items on this list, I am usually back on track and creating again. Even if it's not the type of creativity I wanted to begin, any motion is good motion. You might find yourself writing one line of a book each day. That is still creating. This is you meeting creativity, and the Muses are supporting you along the way.

How to Recognize Inspiration from Muses

Recognizing inspiration is not the same for everyone, much like knowing you are in the presence of a godd is not the same for every person. What I know to be true is this: inspiration can come from anywhere, but it also requires empty space. A full cup is hard to pour into; a full mind is hard to reorganize.

Here are a few practices that I have found helpful:

Meditation / Clearing the Mind

The first step for me when inviting inspiration is to clear my mind. You might find meditation helpful for this, the practice of slowing down, going inside yourself, and noticing thoughts without attaching yourself to them. It's not about getting quiet as much as it is about teaching yourself you don't have to let every thought stay in your mind all the time. If you don't want to meditate, you can also try breathwork or movement or imagining yourself letting extra thoughts and worries go. Remember, it's not a practice of perfectly removing everything, but of realizing that you can pay attention to some things and let others drift away to make room for what's important to you.

Turn Down (or Off) New Input

Alongside meditation is turning away from new information. When I first did *The Artist's Way* by Julia Cameron, I remember the week that talked about staying away from the news or the internet. This was before I had a smartphone and before I was on the computer all the time, so this wasn't that hard. And even then, I noticed how much more creative I was when I didn't add to the noise in my head. Even taking a day a week or a few hours a day to just be with the world and myself is enough to help me re-engage with creative practices. I notice what I want to do instead of what new information motivates me to do. Plus, the fewer outside distractions I have, the calmer I am, which often helps the voices of the Muses become louder.

Create Badly

In the moments when I feel stuck, I write anyway. I write things that will never be seen and may even be deleted completely. But I still write. I still create because when I'm so focused on being good, I'm not focused on making something real or true to myself. When I focus so much on the response to what I create, I am not listening to the Muses or to the things that might be different for me. Sometimes, this means I write for a certain period without stopping just to get things down on paper and to get random thoughts out of the way. I write about my worries, my critics, and my desires. After a while, I return to my authentic self, the one who knows the Muses and knows that pauses in creativity are times to rest and celebrate.

Track Inspiration

When I am feeling down about life, I restart my gratitude journal. I will write down three things every day that I am grateful for. It helps recenter my focus. If inspiration is hard to find, I start to look around in my world for things that inspire me. And these things don't have to cause me to create anything – not at all. They just are things that make me feel something, that evoke an experience or a reaction. Today I was inspired by...the sound of the wind on the leaves. The light of the dawn as it stretched across the window. Today I was inspired by the buzz of the light and how it changed as I moved around the room.

Inspiration is everywhere, even if it's not loud and dramatic. Once you begin these practices, you might notice your body feels a certain way when it is inspired. Write that down. Remember that feeling. Chase that feeling. That is the Muses.

Creating Rituals for the Muses

In the next section is a ritual that asks for the support of the Muses, and this outline can be updated for any ritual you might want to offer to them as a group or singularly. Before we get to that, I wanted to offer a few not-as-rigid possibilities too. After all, creativity goes hand in hand with inspiration.

You might have an idea of what you want a Muses ritual to focus on, e.g., calling in inspiration, working with a certain Muse, asking for help with creative blocks, removing obstacles to expression, rewriting negative inner critic stories, etc. If you have more than one idea, I encourage you to write them all down on slips of paper. Put them aside.

Next, think about the kind of ritual you might want, e.g., dance party, art making, candle magick, spellwork to break curses, etc. Write down these options on paper.

Finally, think about whether you want one Muse or more than one, or you're not sure. Write down the Muses name(s) on slips of paper. Or just have one for the group of Muses.

Close your eyes and choose one slip of paper from each pile. This is even more fun when you have a group that comes up with other ritual elements, e.g., ritual location, day, time, snacks to bring, etc.

Whatever you choose (or whatever the group chooses), create that ritual. See how you are inspired by the possibilities and how they impact each other. Not only is this a good practice for making magick with the Muses, but it can also be a fun practice for when you feel stuck in your creative process. Maybe the next time you have a block, you think about the things standing in your way (write those down), the Muses that could help (write those down), and the kind of ritual (serious hex breaking, karaoke fest, altar building with natural things, et. (write those down). Pick the papers that call to you and move through that ritual and move through the stuck place in ritual space.

Practice: Asking for the Muses' Support

> "For the poet [Homer], this invocation is not just a formal convention; it is a serious act of piety, because the account he is about to give is a poetical tour de force, not only of memory but of skill in fitting proper names and place-names into a metrical pattern" (Lefkowitz 59).

Before he writes the story of the leaders of the Greek army, Homer asks the Muses for their support as Homer has read other stories and seen the downfall of those who deemed themselves more knowledgeable than the godds.

This is not to say you must be stoic or grin-less when working with the Muses. They often sing and dance and do not need such emotionless reverence. The Muses do not suffer fools and want the person calling them to be truthful in their request. Knowing the petition's depth, the Muses can make the best decision possible to offer their guidance and inspiration.

There are many ways to ask the Muses for help, and they often look like other rituals. You can create sacred space, invoke them into the place, ask for their help, and thank them for any wisdom or blessings they might have to offer.

You might also want to follow a Greek ritual format (noting that there are differences of opinion on the order of these pieces). As with rituals in ancient Greece, they typically began with an offering to Hestia, who was the hearth of all homes and all families.

Preparations: Prepare your mind and body by grounding and being clear in what you want to ask the Muses.

Procession: You might find a way to move in reverence to a space that is set up to celebrate the Muses, e.g., an altar space, a special place in nature, etc.

Cleansing & Purification: Take a bowl of water and cleanse your hands and forehead, and anywhere else you want to cleanse. I like to put water on my heart and along my throat.

Hymns to the Muses: In many rituals, there is a space for the Muses to be celebrated with Homeric or Orphic hymns.

Offering / Sacrifice: It will be wise to bring an offering to the Muses, allowing them to see that you want to give something in return for their wisdom. This might not be a physical item, as it can also be your time, your attention, and your intention to move ahead in some creative project.

Prayer (Invocation): This is where you can create a prayer to the Muses to call them fully into a space where they are welcome, you are grounded and cleansed, and there is an offering. Here, you can also call to the Muses about what you request of them or what you might ask of them.

Libations: When you feel that you have received what you will from the Muses, you can choose to drink some celebratory drink with them, making sure to offer some to Hestia and to the Muses before you drink.

Gratitude: After the celebration, be sure to give your thanks and if you want to make any more promises to the Muses, you can do that here. Be sure to follow through on your promises.

Chapter 7

Modern Day Muses

Mnemosyne was smitten with astonishment when she heard honey-voiced Sappho, wondering if men possess a tenth Muse.

Antipater of Sidon, The Greek Anthology: Hellenistic Epigrams, 9.66, edited by W.R. Paton

Some say the Muses are nine, but how carelessly! Look at the tenth, Sappho from Lesbos.

Plato, The Greek Anthology: Hellenistic Epigrams, 9.506, edited by W.R. Paton

A Greek poet known for her lyric poetry and the fragments that survived, Sappho created poems meant to be sung, often speaking of love and longing. While she is said to have written 10,000 lines of poetry, only about 650 survived. *Ode to Aphrodite* is one poem that survived mostly intact, while many translations of her work show how one word was left of other lines.[46]

As a writer, I know when the Muses arrive. Or, at least, I know how inspiration arrives for me. I get a feeling in my body, a warm rush that can be interpreted in a few ways. Sometimes, anger burns at the base of my throat and comes armed with all my failings and worries. Sometimes, inspiration arrives alongside insomnia, asking me to watch the darkness of night stretch across the room where I can only think the thoughts that travel like shadows, moving me from knowing to unknowing and back again.

Sometimes, I interpret the rush of blood in my chest as fear. And perhaps that's true. Creativity can be scary. To bring something into being is a terrifying act. To birth something from the imagination is a sort of confession. It's a whisper or a scream into the world: This is what I think. This is the sense I have made of a moment, an idea, an offhand remark, an argument, a story, a relationship, this life.

I hold a few things at the same time here. I believe I am inspired by something beyond me, like the Muses. I also believe that I am inspiring myself with the places I've been, the people I've met, and the things I have learned. In my life, I have collected pieces that inform my inspired moments.

Inspiration is reaching out to others and finding it within myself. In either case, it requires an opening. It requires belief in something I do not know yet. It requires trusting and daring and courage and hope.

What Defines a Muse?

To me, a Muse is an inspiration, those who inspire action, even the smallest step or movement toward revelation. With that in mind, I would expand modern Muses to include non-humans because I have been inspired by the wild and wondrous Earth. My cats have inspired me. I have been inspired by the lean of a tree and the temperature of the wind. I have found inspiration in the shift of seasons and how my skin feels in different cities at different times.

For many, the Muses inspire creatives and artists, which might be limiting. After all, I don't think you need to be an 'artist' or a 'writer' to engage with the Muses. The Muses might inspire you to try on a new life, to move toward a larger dream, and to know your power in a world that needs your unique self. And in these inspired movements, you might become the Muse to another. Or even to yourself.

Inspirational & Influential People & Places

I know that naming modern Muses could be its own book or series, so I offer these as a starting point for conversation. Perhaps I offer this short list as inspiration for you to recognize and name the Muses you already know in your life or those you want to know better.

Who inspires you? Why?
Who provokes you? (Not all inspiration is meant to be followed; some is meant to be reacted to.)
What or who offers you new insights?
How has your creativity changed because of what you've experienced?
What has someone said that caused you to think differently?
Is there something you learned that completely changed the way you see the world?
How have you inspired others with your actions?
(How do you hope to inspire others?)

CALLIOPE / Alok Vaid Menon – Nonbinary writer, poet, and performance artist whose work challenges narratives around gender, reductive categorization across humans and experiences, and self-expression.[47]

CLIO / bell hooks – Queer American author, social critic, and poet who wrote influential books on the black experience, feminism, patriarchy, sexuality, and more.[48]

ERATO / Audre Lorde – Intersectional feminist, activist, poet, lesbian, and professor who wrote about "civil rights, feminism, lesbianism, illness, disability, and the exploration of Black female identity."[49]

EUTERPE / Janelle Monáe – Singer, rapper, songwriter, and nonbinary actress who has received ten Grammy nominations, a Screen Actors Guild Award, and American Society of Composers, Authors and Publishers Vanguard Award.[50]

MELPOMENE / Phoebe Bridgers[51] – American songwriter, singer, and musician who writes songs with melancholic themes.

POLYHYMNIA / Sophie Strand – Per her website[52]: "Sophie Strand is a writer based in the Hudson Valley who focuses on the intersection of spirituality, storytelling, and ecology."

TERPSICHORE / Beyoncé[53] – American singer and songwriter who competed in singing and dancing contests as a small child before joining Destiny's Child and transitioning into the success of her solo career.

THAILA / Marsha P. Johnson – Gay rights activist and self-proclaimed drag queen who was one of the leaders at the Stonewall uprising.[54]

URANIA / Chani Nicholas – Canadian astrologer and activist.

I would extend a list of the Muses beyond humans born in North America and beyond human figures, but as I am US-based, I focused on those.

Practice: Noticing Inspiration in Daily Life

The Muses don't have to be just people or the beings in myths. Just like Iris is a goddess who might arrive in the form you would best recognize and understand, I wonder if the Muses might arrive as places that welcome you and offer you inspiration in the ways only they can.

- An ocean
- The tree next to your school
- That calla lily that blooms every February
- A hidden path between the sidewalks of a neighborhood

- The color of the sky
- The way the moon moves across the sky
- A feather
- The way someone's body moves toward you
- The slant of the floor
- The way light falls through stained glass

A practice that can help is writing down everything that has inspired you each day. You might write about a cup of coffee that reflected the light a certain way. You might also notice how someone in your life has a voice that relaxes you. Or there may be a place on your drive to work that always helps when you need a good idea or a solution.

Think beyond people and stories. Allow yourself to be inspired. And share those inspirations with others to see how you might incite creativity, joy, delight, awe, and wonder.

What do these places feel like?
What stories could you tell of them?
How might you explain natural occurrences in a poem or a sculpture?
Why do you think _________ happens?
Is there another way to describe the shadows?
If you had to describe something to someone without any frame of reference, how would you do that?
Can you sing a song to the land?
What might the land sing back to you?

My witchcraft practice constantly reminds me that I am not separate from the Earth; I am Earth, too. And because of that, what I see as inspiring in the world can be what I see as inspiring in myself and others.

Practice: Taking on the Mind of a Muse

I am my own muse.
I am the subject I know best.
The subject I want to know better.

Frida Kahlo

Maybe Muses are Muses and people are Muses and places or moments are Muses. And maybe you can be a Muse too. Maybe you already are. Even if you never know it, you have inspired people in your life to do things differently. While you may not like how you have inspired people at times, your presence in the world has an impact.

To take this a little further, I encourage you to step into the mind of a Muse. You will need something that inspires you, a physical object that can represent inspiration for you. I might grab a book of Sappho's poetry, but you might have a seashell or a crystal. I invite you to find something that can act as a Muse. And you can repeat this exercise with other items in the future.

Once you have this item, I invite you to close your eyes and feel that item in your hand. You can also look at the items and notice everything you can about it. If this is an item from a particular time or moment of your life, travel back in your mind to that time. What did it feel like? What did you feel like? What happened? What is powerful for you about this memory?

When you feel you are connected strongly to this item, envision the item's energy begin to travel along your skin from your fingertips to your forearms, to your shoulders and to your heart. Notice how this inspiration makes you feel and how it enters your thoughts. This might be a moment just to see what you notice happening in your body and mind. Take time there.

You can also use this time to ask yourself what inspiration this item might have for you. What does this item have to tell you about your life and your direction? What does this item want to tell you about inspiration or creativity? What does this item have to share?

Sometimes, it can help to have a specific question in mind before allowing the item's energy to travel along your body. Still, I notice that when I am open to whatever comes, this is also powerful.

Take time to see what happens and what you might learn from this item. When you are ready to be done, allow the energy to travel back out of your body and back into the item. Move the item away from you so you are no longer connected. This is a good time to write down anything you may have learned or record anything in a voice note. You might also respond with a drawing or some other creative expression.

When you step into being the Muse, what do you offer to yourself? Once you are comfortable, you might also hold onto an item for another person and speak from the energy of that item to answer questions another person might have.

Chapter 8

Cultivating a Relationship with the Muses

> *...for...speak...*
> *(Sing of) the bride with her beautiful feet*
> *...the violet-robed daughter [Artemis] of Zeus*
> *... putting aside anger...violet-robed...*
> *(Hither,) holy Graces and Pierian Muses*
> *when...song(s)...the mind...*
> *...hearing a clear song...*
> *...bridegroom, for annoying (to?) companions...*
> *...her hair, putting down the lyre...*
>
> Fragment 103, Sappho, Greek Lyric I,
> translated by David A. Campbell

The Muses enter the room, singing as they are asked. They enter with a song that lights up the air and allows the world to become a more beautiful place, if only for a moment. While the spaces in the poem's fragments might offer some potential for the song to be annoying and thus the need for the lyre to be put down, it isn't clear. I, for one, envision the Muses as a gift to this moment.

But isn't it like this for every relationship? There are interpretations of creativity, just as there are interpretations of love. Thus, building relationships with anyone, including the Muses, will be unique to the one seeking out their presence.

Altar & Creative Space

Like other godds, the Muses delight in creation and adoration, so building an altar is a way to begin to invite them into your space. This altar might include imagery of each Muses, or some, or their symbols and instruments. You might also include:

Poetry books
Books about writing
Records or CDs
Musical instruments
Astrology charts
Comedy and tragedy masks
Pamphlets from plays

I would also encourage you to consider dedicating any craft or creative space to the Muses. This can serve as an extra temple for the Muses or the temple itself. Because the Muses delight in the activity of creation, each time you create in a space, you celebrate their energy and their inspiration. And if you are not someone who wants to be 'out' in your magickal practice, just naming a creative space, bag, tools, etc. can be the way you have an altar out in the open, as well as your practice out in the open.

Learning & Listening

Reading books and source material about the Muses is another way to begin to relate to the Muses more deeply. While the Muses tend to be referenced in writings versus having much said about them, you can find their energy mentioned across genres. Some of the writings are shared in the previous Stories section, but I invite you to seek out other translations of the selections so you can see what different translators found in the language.

Finding books of Greek poetry and mythology source texts in audio form can also be helpful to connect, even if you're unable to understand each word. I like to imagine the influence of the Muses on the stories that have become treasured in magickal and mystical circles. After all, the result of inspiration can be attributed to the Muses. Their influence can be felt and understood without needing to be prescriptive about their involvement.

As I referenced at the beginning, you might seek out modern authors and creators who talk about their muses, the Muses, and other sources of inspiration.

Creating with the Muses

Whether the space is dedicated to the Muses or not, creating is an act of communion with the Muses. And while you might choose to work on a project or an art you already enjoy, there is something to be said for allowing inspiration to take you in new directions.

I encourage you to seek out activities that are outside of your comfort zone. For example, perhaps you try to write when you usually dance. Or you choose to sing when you would usually review the current astrology. You might set aside time to be with inspiration or a certain Muse or all of them.

A practice that can help is one that I've adapted from my witchcraft tradition. Expanding your awareness to make contact beyond your everyday awareness is a practice. All you need to do is let go or loosen any parts of you connected to what will happen next or what happened before this moment. This could look like breathing out to blow away those connections or using a hand or knife to cut them away.

Once you are not connected, breathe in and blow out as hard as possible. You can do this several times until you have cleared the room or space around you. When the space feels open and wider, you can breathe again to send out your normal-sized awareness. Send it out to the horizon or to the widest part of the room so you have space for inspiration.

You can do this as many times as you like, even breathing out from your toes and from every place of your body, e.g., your knees, your hips, your belly button, your heart, your shoulders, your throat, your eyes, your forehead, and your mouth. Notice how big it feels to be present and wider in this space than before.

In that energy, listen to what inspiration might offer to you. And it might not be a word or a phrase, so just follow your instincts. Do you want to move to another chair? Do that. Do you want to paint? Do that. Follow whatever you notice in the space you're in. What you're doing is answering the call of inspiration and allowing it to guide you. The more you trust in something coming, the more will arrive.

If you feel the energy is drifting or shrinking back in, you can breathe out again and again. If you notice you are not feeling as connected, you can also take breaths in to pull the space back to yourself. You can come back to the size of your body and your everyday experience and wrap up the time.

What often happens is the more you do this, the easier it is to widen your awareness and come into the present moment. You might learn to do this anywhere you are and at any time. The Muses know when they are invited and may be waiting for you once they trust you are ready for them too.

Reciprocation & Relationship

Working with some deities can be challenging as you need to get to know them to understand what they might want from the relationship you build. The Muses are different, as they are the inspiration for the things you might create – and those things are the offerings back to them, as much as they are offerings to others in the world. You can best reciprocate the Muses' blessings by creating.

This should not be construed as advice to produce more and more. (That is capitalism's game.) Instead, creating is about taking the time to make something, sing something, move your body, or whatever you want because you want to. Perhaps even because you need to do it. And creation can take time and effort. It might not be done in one sitting or one year. For example, if you connect with Erato to create a book of love poetry, you may not complete this in a lifetime. However, the creation itself is the reciprocation that builds the relationship.

Relationships require giving and receiving, paying attention, and acting on information. Much like any relationship in your life now, the Muses want these things, too. And for your effort, they offer inspiration to guide you.

What can you offer?
What can you offer to the Muses?
What can you vow to the Muses?

One practice I often see among creative folks I know is sharing their art with others. This can be shared in physical spaces, including group art sessions or casual art shows. This can be sharing creative expressions on social media, in a text message, or in conversations.

The Muses might offer inspiration, but what do you do with that gift? This gift is meant to be passed on, shared, and celebrated. After all, when you share creative works, you not only share your expression, but you will inspire someone else, too. Though you might never see the impact of your inspiration, what you share does have an impact. That is a relationship, too, the one between what is created and what is enjoyed. A reciprocal partnership that incites more and more.

One Muse? Many Muses?

When choosing to work with the Muses, you may have already begun to connect with one Muse more than another. Or you may be interested in working with the Muses as a whole group. At this point, I encourage you to consider your goals in your practice with them.

- What is the intention?
- What do you want from this relationship?
- What do you bring to this relationship?
- What are you willing to commit to?
- What do you believe the Muses have to offer you?

The more you can consider your intentions and boundaries, the more you can define your desired relationship. And you can always change your mind later if that feels right.

For the beginner who is nervous about making the 'wrong' choice, you might consider working with the Muses as a group. Once you become comfortable with those practices, you can focus on one (or more) Muses who might hold energies of greater interest.

If you want to work with the Muses as individuals, here are some ideas to get started.

Calliope, Epic Poetry

- Write a poem about the story of your life.
- Read epic poems aloud to a friend.
- Listen to audiobooks of epic poems, e.g., *The Odyssey, The Iliad.*

Clio, History

- Take time to learn about your family history.
- Research the history of the land you live on.
- Engage critical thinking when reading about history; consider other perspectives and narratives beyond those you learned in school.

Erato, Love Poetry

- Write a love poem to yourself and read it aloud while looking in a mirror.

- Read Sappho's poetry (or another poet's love poetry).
- Create a playlist of songs about love and dance to it.

Euterpe, Music

- Build playlists for special occasions or moods.
- Go into nature and find music in the landscape, animals, weather, etc.
- Find a musical instrument and try to play it.

Melpomene, Tragedy

- Watch or read a tragedy play.
- Perform a scene of tragedy in a mirror with yourself.
- Tell someone the story of a memorable life tragedy.

Polyhymnia, Sacred Poetry

- Read a book of ecstatic poetry, e.g., Hafiz, Rumi.
- Listen to wordless spiritual or New Age-type music and write a poem as you are inspired.
- Take a song you love and read it to yourself like a spoken word poet.

Terpsichore, Dance

- Dance to your favorite song or album or playlist.
- Move your body in rhythm to how you want your day to feel.
- Find someone who will dance with you in public.

Thalia, Comedy

- Talk to a person who always makes you laugh.

- Watch a funny movie or comedy show.
- Collect some 'dad jokes' and tell them to your friends.

Urania, Astronomy

- Read your horoscope every day.
- Learn about how the stars move in the sky where you live.
- Spend time looking up at the sky after dark.

These ideas are meant to inspire you if you need somewhere to start. But you can do whatever seems best to work with any of these Muses. After all, they are the purveyors of inspiration, so while you might think about love poetry with Erato, they might also inspire you to trace words of love on the bark of a tree or the back of a lover. Though tragedy might be what Melpomene is connected to, they might also nudge you toward celebrating the parts of your life when things went horribly wrong as they brought you to something better.

It goes without saying, but...be creative with your Muses.

Moving On with the Muses

If you have worked with one Muse and want to move on to another, this is perfectly reasonable. What I might offer, however, is that you create a ritual of gratitude for the time you spent together. This will help acknowledge this interaction's gifts and step away gracefully. After all, you may want to return to this Muse, and having a no-drama ending is good for any relationship.

Gratitude

Giving thanks is a simple and necessary ritual. You might make a special altar or space with things that remind you of the Muse, as well as creations that came from your time together. In this space, tell the Muse how thankful you are for their support and inspiration. This doesn't have to be complicated or formal, unless that is reflective of your relationship.

Display, Share, or Gift Creations

It's wise to make sure any creations or results of your time together are displayed or shared in some way. Let their inspiration flow into the world. You might want to give a creation to someone and let them know what inspired it. When you allow the creativity to flow, it extends the reach of the Muse and can encourage someone else to seek their guidance.

Praise the Muse

You may also want to praise the Muse by talking about them or chanting their name in celebration. Some might want to have a tattoo of their name or instrument/focus on a body part. Others might have a piece of jewelry that is inspired by them. I have found stickers for the Muses to place where I can see them and remember them fondly. Ongoing attention can serve as praise, too.

I don't say this lightly and don't like telling readers what to do, but I don't think the Muses are beings that ever go away. They linger in the background, like beneficent ancestors, waiting to see if you need anything. The Muses are supportive and want their inspiration to find its place in the world.

Practice: Ritual for Dedication to the Muses

While you may not see yourself as a creative person (yet), I believe dedicating to the Muses is a worthwhile rite. By honoring those who might offer insight and inspiration, you connect more fully to those who likely already whisper things in your ear. This rite can help increase the volume and allow you to hear things more clearly.

You will need:

Altar items for the Muse or Muses you want to honor
Candle of any color that suits you and your creativity
Items for creative play, e.g., fingerpaints, a journal and pen, musical instrument, clay, poetry, etc.
Journal and pen (if you didn't choose that for your playtime)

Find a place where you will not be disturbed, such as a separate room or outside where you feel safe and comfortable. In that space, set up an altar to the Muse or Muses you want to honor here. I like cleaning the space and ground before casting a circle and calling in the elements and deities.

You can cast a circle here and call in elements or allies. Once you have the beings called in, it's time to invite the Muse or Muses you want to call in. While sometimes it's a good idea to prepare something beforehand, and you can undoubtedly create an invocation beforehand, I encourage you to follow your intuition for this invocation. Talk to the Muses about what you know about them, what is wonderful about them, and what stories have been told about them. Then, introduce who you are and what you are looking for. Share what you have to offer this relationship and what you can do in return for their grace and blessing.

Once you feel the Muse(s) in the space with you, stop and wait for them to influence your next action. Follow what you think is being asked of you and step into a creative play space with the items you brought. Take time to create and follow what you believe the Muse(s) inspire you to do.

Stay in this creative space as long as you feel it is good. Once you are complete, light the candle and move the light of the candle around what you have created. Talk to the Muse(s) about what you have done and what they have inspired. Tell them what you felt in your body and what you noticed about their ideas. Once you have shown it in detail, wait to see how the Muse(s) might respond.

After you feel a response, you can then ask to commit to them for a certain time period of inspiration and play. Wait to hear their answer and any advice they might have to offer. While you might not get a dramatic response, trust you will know if this is not a good relationship to commit to. (And if this is the case, stop the ritual, thank the Muses, the allies, the elements, and open the circle. Come back to the ritual at another time.)

When you feel the blessing, thank the Muses and reaffirm what you have to offer to them. You might repeat their name(s) to seal the rite and devoke them and anything else you might have invoked.

If you created a thing during the ritual, place that on the altar or in a central place where you can reflect on it. If you did not create a thing, but rather a song or a dance, remember that by writing it down in your journal, along with anything else you learned from the Muse(s).

Follow up on your promises. Take care of this relationship. Let yourself be inspired again and again.

Conclusion

The root of the word 'Muses' is also the root of 'museum,' moving from the Greek word 'mousa' (Muses) to the Greek word 'mouseion' (seat of the Muses) to museum in the early 17th century.[55] When I think of a museum, I think of it as a place where inspiration is displayed in many forms. This is a place of reverence and a place to ask questions about who can ever claim to own the gifts of the Muses.

It is wise to be reminded now that the Muses are the daughters of Power (Zeus) and Mnemosyne (Memory). These goddesses bring forward these energies too, and we might remember that who holds power often holds certain memories – or the memories that best serve them. Some things are lost to time, or, perhaps, misplaced to suit a more 'favorable' story.

> "Nowadays, we tend to think it's enough to create museums and libraries to fulfill the function of Memory. We maintain archives, train historians, and encourage groups to preserve their common heritage and invest in computers with enormous memory banks. Of course, these are all necessary, but literacy – and, even more, computer literacy – can make us all victims of amnesia" (Paris 119).

The Muses can offer so much to us as individuals and so much more to the collective. Lefkowitz points out that Hesiod may have learned his song from the Muses and was even given a staff and named a poet (14-15). With their admittance of knowing the difference between what is true and what is not true, they are not necessarily offering a warning about the inspiration they provide, but rather a reminder that a human is not a godd and is therefore unable to discern what is true from what is not true.

It is up to us to learn and know and share. What we say may not be understood or received or even celebrated, but what we offer to the world, we offer to the next new idea, the next solution, the next generation, and the next story.

With that in mind, let us remember to sing first and last of the Muses, as they have reminded Hesiod from the start.

Muses of Memory and Power,
We honor you,
Muses of Memory and Power,
We celebrate you,
Muses of Memory and Power,
We thank you.

Calliope, thank for the harmonies of higher keys,
Clio, thank you for the context of history and celebrations,
Erato, thank you for the poetry of desire and longing,
Euterpe, thank you for the breath that makes music and delight,
Melpomene, thank you for the honoring of loss with song,
Polyhymnia, thank you for making words sacred and holy,
Terpsichore, thank you for the way you move and invoke melodies,
Thalia, thank you for levity and the honoring of joy,
Urania, thank you for showing us the stars and the heavens, where Love lives.
We thank you sweet Muses
For inspirations received,
For inspirations still on their way,
May we discern your gifts,
May we share your wisdom,
May we embody your poetry,
May we become inspiration too,
May our hearts always remember
The daughters of Memory and Power.

Hail Calliope!
Hail Clio!
Hail Erato!
Hail Euterpe!
Hail Melpomene!
Hail Polyhymnia!
Hail Terpsichore!
Hail Thalia!
Hail Urania!

Hail the Muses!

Endnotes

1. Author Note: A Greek writer or poet always began their writing with an invocation to the Muses.
2. Not Greek, *estampie* means sound, or the creation of a lovely sound as the Muses walked to Zeus. https://www.merriam-webster.com/dictionary/estampie#:~:text=%3A%20a%20usually%20textless%2C%20monophonic%20musical,that%20probably%20accompanied%20a%20dance
3. Επιστήμη & Ζωή. Greece: CHATZIAKOVOU S.A. Vol.13, p.151.
4. Fragment 67, Diodorus Siculus 4. 7. 1, translated by Charles Henry Oldfather.
5. Praxilla of Sicyon, Fragment 3, translated by David Campbell.
6. Mimnermus, Fragment 13, translated by David Gerber.
7. https://historycooperative.org/muses/
8. https://www.greekmyths-greekmythology.com/nine-muses-in-greek-mythology/
9. Gardner, James. The faiths of the world; an account of all religions and religious sects, their doctrines, rites, ceremonies, and customs. Pg 639.
10. https://en.wikipedia.org/wiki/Pegasides
11. https://en.wikipedia.org/wiki/Aganippe_(naiad)
12. https://www.britannica.com/topic/Castalia
13. https://en.wikipedia.org/wiki/Leibethra
14. https://en.wikipedia.org/wiki/Pegasides
15. https://www.britannica.com/topic/Muse-Greek-mythology
16. Polymatheia was named for "Much Learning," https://www.britannica.com/topic/Muse-Greek-mythology
17. Bell, Robert E. *Women of Classical Mythology, A biographical dictionary*.

18. Bell, Robert E. *Women of Classical Mythology, A biographical dictionary.*
19. https://www.theoi.com/Titan/Mousai.html
20. Tzetzes, Scholia in Hesiodi Opera 1.23
21. https://www.greeklegendsandmyths.com/the-elder-muses.html
22. H. Munro Chadwick and Nora K. Chadwick. *The Growth of Literature.*
23. Karl Kerényi: *The Gods of the Greeks,* Pg. 104 and note 284
24. William Smith, editor. *A Dictionary of Greek and Roman Biography and Mythology.*
25. Mneme might also be Mnemosyne, the Titan goddess.
26. Diodorus Siculus, 4.7.1–2
27. https://www.getty.edu/art/collection/object/103R7F
28. Orphic Hymn XXXIII to Apollo, translated by Thomas Taylor.
29. Orphic Hymn XXXIV to Apollo, translated by Thomas Taylor.
30. https://www.perseus.tufts.edu/hopper/text?doc=Perseus%3Atext%3A1999.01.0166%3Abook%3D2%3Apage%3D653
31. https://www.theoi.com/Ouranios/MousaiApollonides.html
32. A device that measured time by the flow of water. https://www.britannica.com/technology/clepsydra
33. https://www.britannica.com/topic/Euterpe-Muse
34. https://historycooperative.org/muses/
35. Godwin, Joscelyn. *The Pagan Dream of the Renaissance.*
36. The Library of Greek Mythology. Apollodorus, 1.3.3
37. https://www.britannica.com/topic/sphinx#ref799746
38. https://en.wikipedia.org/wiki/Theatre_of_the_Oppressed
39. Cicero, *De Natura Deorum* 3. 36, translated by H. Rackham.
40. *Greek Lyric V,* Fragments 1027f, translated by David Campbell.
41. H.L. Jones, editor. *The Geography of Strabo* 9. 2. 25

42. https://www.britannica.com/topic/Muse-Greek-mythology
43. William Smith, William Wayte, and G. E. Marindin, Ed. *A Dictionary of Greek and Roman Antiquities*
44. https://en.wikipedia.org/wiki/Valley_of_the_Muses
45. G. Roux. *Le Val des Muses et les Musees chez les auteurs anciens.*
46. https://en.wikipedia.org/wiki/Sappho
47. https://en.wikipedia.org/wiki/Alok_Vaid-Menon
48. https://en.wikipedia.org/wiki/Bell_hooks
49. https://en.wikipedia.org/wiki/Audre_Lorde
50. https://en.wikipedia.org/wiki/Janelle_Mon%C3%A1e
51. https://en.wikipedia.org/wiki/Phoebe_Bridgers
52. https://sophiestrand.com/
53. https://en.wikipedia.org/wiki/Beyonc%C3%A9
54. https://en.wikipedia.org/wiki/Marsha_P._Johnson
55. https://www.etymonline.com/word/museum

Appendix: Recommended Reading

Albert, Liv. *Greek Mythology: The Gods, Goddesses, and Heroes Handbook*. Adams Media. 2021.

Apollodorus. *The Library of Greek Mythology,* Translated by J.G. Frazer. Oxford University Press. 2017.

Apollodorus. *The Library of Greek Mythology*. Translated by Robin Hard. Oxford University Press. 1997.

Arrien, Angeles. *The Nine Muses: A Mythological Path to Creativity*. Jeremy P. Tarcher/Putnam. 2000.

Athanassakis, Apostolos N. *Theogony, Works and Days, Shield*. Johns Hopkins University Press. 1983.

Batchelor, Stephen. *The Ancient Greeks for Dummies*. For Dummies. 2011.

Bolten, Lesley. *The Everything Classical Mythology Book*. F+W Publications 2002.

Evslin, Bernard. *Gods, Demigods, and Demons: An Encyclopedia of Greek Mythology*. Scholastic Inc. 1975.

Fantham, Elaine, Helene Peet Foley, Natalie Noymel Kampen, Sarah B. Pomeroy, and H. Alan Shapiro. *Women in the Classical World*. Oxford University Press. 1994.

Graves, Robert. *The Greek Myths*. Penguin Books. 1993.

Homer. *The Iliad*. Translated by Emily Wilson. W.W. Norton & Company. 2023.

Impelluso, Lucia. *Myths: Tales of the Greek and Roman Gods*. Abrams. 2008.

Jackson, J.L, editor. *Greek Myths & Legends: Tales of Heroes, Gods & Monsters*. Flame Tree Publishing. 2022.

Johnston, Sarah Iles. *Gods and Mortals: Ancient Greek Myths for Modern Readers*. Princeton University Press. 2023.

Mankey, Jason & Astrea Taylor. *Modern Witchcraft with the Greek Gods: History, Insights & Magickal Practice*. Llewellyn Publications. 2022.

Matyszak, Philip. *The Gods and Goddesses of Greece & Rome*. Thames & Hudson. 2022.

Monaghan, Patricia. *The New Book of Goddesses & Heroines*. Llewellyn Publications. 1997.

Moon, Irisanya. *Pantheon: The Greeks*. Moon Books. 2025.

Parin D'aulaires, Ingri and Edgar. *D'aulaires' Book of Greek Myths*. Bantam Doubleday Dell Publishing Group. 1962.

Powell, Barry B. *Greek Poems to the Gods: Hymns from Home to Proclus*. University of California Press. 2021.

Rayor, Diane J. *The Homeric Hymns: A Translation, with Introduction and Notes*. University of California Press. 2014.

Roebuck, Carl, editor. *The Muses at Work: Arts, Crafts, and Professions in Ancient Greece and Rome*. The MIT Press. 1969.

Rose. H.J. *A Handbook of Greek Mythology*. E.P. Dutton & Co., Inc. 1959.

Bibliography

https://en.wikipedia.org/wiki/Greek_mythology
https://www.theoi.com

Antipater of Sidon / Plato. *The Greek Anthology: Hellenistic Epigrams*, edited by W.R. Paton. Harvard University Press. 1917.

Bell, Robert E. *Women of Classical Mythology, A biographical dictionary*. Oxford University Press. 1993.

Burkert, Walter. *Greek Religion*. Harvard University Press. 1985.

Chadwick, H. Munro and Nora K. Chadwick. *The Growth of Literature*. Cambridge University Press. 2010.

Collective work by scholars and expertise. *Επιστήμη & Ζωή*. Greece: CHATZIAKOVOU S.A. pp. Vol.13, p.151. 1980.

Gardner, James. *The faiths of the world; an account of all religions and religious sects, their doctrines, rites, ceremonies, and customs*. Edinburgh, London: A. Fullarton & Co. 1860.

Godwin, Joscelyn. *The Pagan Dream of the Renaissance*. Weiser Books. 2002.

Goodrich, Norma Lorre. *Priestesses*. Harper Perennial. 1989.

Graziosi, Barbara. *The Gods of Olympus: A History*. Metropolitan Books. 2014.

Grimal, Pierre. *The Penguin Dictionary of Classical Mythology*. Penguin Books, 1991.

Hamilton, Edith. *Mythology*. Little, Brown and Company. 1942.

Harrison, Jane Ellen. *Prolegomena to the Study of Greek Religion*. Princeton University Press. 1991.

Hatab, Lawrence J. *Myth and Philosophy: A Contest of Truths*. Open Court Publishing Company. 1990.

Homer. *The Odyssey*. Translated by Emily Wilson. W.W. Norton & Company. 2017.

Hesiod. *Theogony*. Translated by M.L. West. Oxford University Press. 1988.

Jones, H. L., editor, *The Geography of Strabo*. Harvard University Press; London: William Heinemann, Ltd. 1924.

Kerényi, Karl. *The Gods of the Greeks*. Thames & Hudson, London. 1951.

Lattimore, Richmond. *The Iliad of Homer*. The University of Chicago Press. 2011.

Lefkowitz, Mary. *Greek Gods, Human Lives: What We Can Learn from Myths*. Yale University Press. 2003.

Paris, Ginette. *Pagan Grace: Dionysos, Hermes, and Goddess Memory in Daily Life*. Spring Publications Inc. 1990.

Roberts, Ellie Mackin. *Heroines of Olympus: The Women of Greek Mythology*. Welbeck. 2020.

Roux, G. *Le Val des Muses et les Musees chez les auteurs anciens*, Bulletin de Correspondance Hellenique. 1954.

Smith, William, editor. *A Dictionary of Greek and Roman Biography and Mythology*. Little, Brown, and Company. 1867.

Taylor, Thomas, translator. *The Hymns of Orpheus*. University of Pennsylvania Press, 1792, 1999.

Trzaskoma, Stephen M., Scott R. Smith, and Stephen Brunet. *Anthology of Classical Myth: Primary Sources in Translation*. Hackett Publishing Company. 2016.

Wayte, William and G. E. Marindin, editors. *A Dictionary of Greek and Roman Antiquities*. William Smith, LLD. 1890.

About the Author

Irisanya Moon (she/they) is a priestess, teacher, and initiate in the Reclaiming tradition. She has taught classes and camps worldwide, including in the US, Canada, UK, and Australia. Irisanya writes a Substack newsletter called Heart Magick, which can be found at https://irisanya.substack.com/

You can find out more about Irisanya's writing
and teaching at...
www.irisanyamoon.com

Books by Irisanya Moon...

Earth Spirit
Gaia: Saving Her, Saving Ourselves
Honoring the Wild: Reclaiming Witchcraft & Environmental Activism

Pagan Portals
Reclaiming Witchcraft
Aphrodite – Encountering the Goddess of Love & Beauty & Initiation
Iris – Goddess of the Rainbow and Messenger of the Godds
The Norns – Weavers of Fate and Magick
Artemis – Goddess of the Wild Hunt & Sovereign Heart
Circe – Goddess of Sorcery
Hestia – Goddess of Hearth, Home & Community

Pantheon
The Greeks

Practically Pagan
An Alternative Guide to Health & Well-being

MOON BOOKS

PAGANISM & SHAMANISM

What is Paganism? A religion, a spirituality, an alternative belief system, nature worship? You can find support for all these definitions (and many more) in dictionaries, encyclopaedias, and text books of religion, but subscribe to any one and the truth will evade you. Above all Paganism is a creative pursuit, an encounter with reality, an exploration of meaning and an expression of the soul. Druids, Heathens, Wiccans and others, all contribute their insights and literary riches to the Pagan tradition. Moon Books invites you to begin or to deepen your own encounter, right here, right now.

If you have enjoyed this book, why not tell other readers by posting a review on your preferred book site.

Bestsellers from Moon Books

Pagan Portals Series

The Morrigan
Meeting the Great Queens
Morgan Daimler
Ancient and enigmatic, the Morrigan reaches out to us. On shadowed wings and in raven's call, meet the ancient Irish goddess of war, battle, prophecy, death, sovereignty, and magic.
Paperback: 978-1-78279-833-0 ebook: 978-1-78279-834-7

The Awen Alone
Walking the Path of the Solitary Druid
Joanna van der Hoeven
An introductory guide for the solitary Druid, The Awen Alone will accompany you as you explore, and seek out your own place within the natural world.
Paperback: 978-1-78279-547-6 ebook: 978-1-78279-546-9

Moon Magic
Rachel Patterson
An introduction to working with the phases of the Moon, what they are and how to live in harmony with the lunar year and to utilise all the magical powers it provides.
Paperback: 978-1-78279-281-9 ebook: 978-1-78279-282-6

Hekate
A Devotional
Vivienne Moss
Hekate, Queen of Witches and the Shadow-Lands, haunts the pages of this devotional bringing magic and enchantment into your lives
Paperback: 978-1-78535-161-7 ebook: 978-1-78535-162-4

Bestsellers from Moon Books

Keeping Her Keys
An Introduction to Hekate's Modern Witchcraft
Cyndi Brannen
Blending Hekate, witchcraft and personal development together to create a powerful new magickal perspective.
Paperback: 978-1-78904-075-3 ebook 978-1-78904-076-0

Journey to the Dark Goddess
How to Return to Your Soul
Jane Meredith
Discover the powerful secrets of the Dark Goddess and transform your depression, grief and pain into healing and integration.
Paperback: 978-1-84694-677-6 ebook: 978-1-78099-223-5

Shamanic Reiki
Expanded Ways of Working with Universal Life Force Energy
Llyn Roberts, Robert Levy
Shamanism and Reiki are each powerful ways of healing; together, their power multiplies. Shamanic Reiki introduces techniques to help healers and Reiki practitioners tap ancient healing wisdom.
Paperback: 978-1-84694-037-8 ebook: 978-1-84694-650-9

Southern Cunning
Folkloric Witchcraft in the American South
Aaron Oberon
Modern witchcraft with a Southern flair, this book is a journey through the folklore of the American South and a look at the power these stories hold for modern witches.
Paperback: 978-1-78904-196-5 ebook: 978-1-78904-197-2

Readers of ebooks can buy or view any of these bestsellers by clicking on the live link in the title. Most titles are published in paperback and as an ebook. Paperbacks are available in traditional bookshops. Both print and ebook formats are available online.

Find more titles and sign up to our readers' newsletter www.collectiveinkbooks.com/paganism

For video content, author interviews and more, please subscribe to our YouTube channel.

MoonBooksPublishing

Follow us on social media for book news, promotions and more:

Facebook: Moon Books

Instagram: @MoonBooksCI

X: @MoonBooksCI

TikTok: @MoonBooksCI